LETTERING ARTS

Joanne Fink
Judy Kastin

PBC

Library of Applied Design

An Imprint of

P B C   I N T E R N A T I O N A L,   I N C.

For my good friend Steve — who saw it in proof form — and approved! Best always, Joanne

Distributor to the book trade in the United States and Canada:
Rizzoli International Publications Inc.
300 Park Avenue South
New York, NY 10010

Distributor to the art trade in the United States and Canada:
PBC International, Inc.
One School Street
Glen Cove, NY 11542

Distributor throughout the rest of the world:
Hearst Books International
1350 Avenue of the Americas
New York, NY 10019

Library of Congress Cataloging-in-publication Data

Fink, Joanne. 1959–
    Lettering arts / by Joanne Fink and Judy Kastin.
        p.   cm. — (Library of applied design)
    Includes bibliographical references and index
    ISBN 0-86636-225-8   ISBN 0-86636-285-1 (pbk)
    1. Lettering. I. Kastin, Judy. II. Title. III. Series.
NK3600.F54 1993
745.6'1—dc20   93-1615
                                               CIP

Note: All measurements referred to herein are given in
inches unless otherwise indicated.

CAVEAT - Extensive research has gone into the creation of this book.
Information on each piece and permission to publish were supplied by the artist.
The authors have made every effort to insure the
accuracy of this manuscript.

Color separation, printing and binding by
Dai Nippon Printing Group

Printed in Hong Kong

10 9 8 7 6 5 4 3 2 1

To everyone who shares our joy in lettering,
especially our calligraphic friends, teachers and students
—past, present and future.

Joanne Fink and Judy Kastin

For my ever-patient family:
Jeffrey, Matthew, Mom and Dad, with love.
JBK

For my inspiring teacher, Sheila Waters,
and for my understanding family, with love.
JCF

TABLE OF CONTENTS

FOREWORD

My early studies of calligraphy began in art school in England, 45 years ago, at a time when the only calligraphic manuals available for study were Edward Johnston's famous *Writing and Illuminating and Lettering*, Graily Hewitt's *Lettering*, and the anthology *Lettering of Today*. Because those sources gave sound guidance they aided good teachers, trained by Johnston, to produce a generation of professional calligraphers who were able to undertake the formal works commissioned in the post–World War II period, including Rolls of Honour, presentation scrolls, framed speeches and awards, etc. By that time the influence of calligraphy had filtered into the commercial fields of advertising and publishing to a limited extent. Hand lettering of any kind was expected to be highly finished with little freedom allowed, let alone with the deliberate rough edges so popular today.

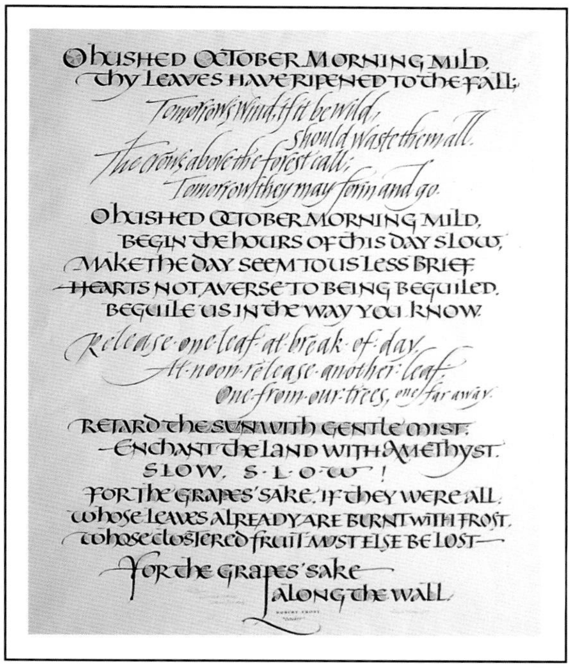

Foremost among the loosening influences has been that of German calligraphers. Contemporary with the pioneer Johnston in England, Rudolf Koch, followed by Rudolf von Larisch and Ernst Schneidler led a freer, more expressionistic movement, and the combination of these English and German traditions has been the major influence on calligraphy in Europe and America, from the thirties to the present.

For many years calligraphy held a lowly position in the graphic scene in the Western world; wider recognition of its value has been gradual. However, in the last 25 years attitudes seem to have changed, so that the general public is now more aware of the word "calligraphy" (even if viewer perception is limited to "that fancy writing"), because it is now seen everywhere.

Throughout the past five decades some anthologies of fine quality and usefulness have appeared and it is necessary and important that aspiring calligraphers, lettering designers, type designers, typographers and graphic artists in general should have good current models available for inspiration and guidance. So I welcome *Lettering Arts*, as an important anthology because it contains a representative selection of the finest quality work being produced today. It showcases a full spectrum of variety of uses, from trendy and ephemeral to classical and timeless, according to the original requirement for each individual piece. It does not seek to make comparisons of value of importance, but lets each category of work show its own merits. In other words, it is not helpful to think in terms of these categories as rungs on a ladder of worthiness, the "fine art" category at the top, but rather as stations along a track, each having its own intrinsic worth and meaning. A beautifully designed invitation, certificate or logo is just as worthy in its own right as an interpretation of an author's words or a poet's thoughts or a piece of "art for art's sake" expressionism.

Sheila Waters, "October," 1985. Poem by Robert Frost.

Because this collection is international in scope, just as the fraternity of those who practice calligraphy and lettering is international, it should have wide usefulness for this and for the coming generations of lettering designers and also for art directors and others who commission their work.

Sheila Waters
Gaithersburg, Maryland

Internationally known calligraphic artist Sheila Waters was born in England, trained at the Royal College of Art and was elected a Fellow of the prestigious London Society of Scribes and Illuminators in 1951. In 1971 she moved to the United States and in 1972 began the calligraphic program for the Smithsonian Institution Associates. She is the founding president and first honorary lifetime member of the Washington Calligraphers Guild. Her work is owned by royalty, private collections, museums and institutions throughout the world.

INTRODUCTION

Lettering Arts showcases some of the best work that has been created in the international world of lettering in recent years. Over 200 artists submitted approximately 2,500 pieces to be considered for inclusion in this book. Almost 300 outstanding examples were selected, many of which are being published for the first time. A surprising number of writing implements—everything from traditional quills, pens and brushes to ruling pens and popsicle sticks—have been used to create the pieces in this book. *Lettering Arts* intends to awaken a general sensitivity to the possibilities and beauty of hand-crafted letterforms, and to excite and inspire artists working in the lettering design field.

Calligraphy has a rich history. Through the centuries numerous alphabet styles evolved in handwritten manuscripts. Many of these styles were revived by Edward Johnston, the English pioneer of the twentieth-century calligraphy movement. His treatise, *Writing & Illuminating & Lettering*, published in 1906, reintroduced the use of the broad-edged pen and sparked a vibrant new interest in the calligraphic arts. Johnston's students founded the London based Society of Scribes and Illuminators in 1921. In the United States lettering classes were offered at the college level by Paul Standard, Lloyd Reynolds, James Hayes, Father Edward M. Catitch and Arnold Bank, among others. From Germany, Hermann Zapf is considered to be one of the most important figures in twentieth-century calligraphy and type design. The contributions of these noted scribes have inspired future generations of calligraphers.

In the late 1960s Donald Jackson, one of England's leading scribes, encouraged the growth of American calligraphy societies during his lecture tours. These groups have become the primary source of calligraphic education in the United States, by sponsoring workshops, programs, and publications for their members. Today there are more than one hundred societies devoted to the calligraphic arts. (See Appendix I for a list of some of the major societies.)

Adult education classes and instructional books offer prospective students an introduction to calligraphy and the study of historical manuscripts and contemporary alphabets. Those interested in more extensive training, and in the work of today's leading international scribes, attend workshops sponsored by local groups. In addition to teaching short workshops, noted authorities Sheila Waters, Reggie Ezell, Peter Thornton and other talented teachers offer in-depth or long-term courses. Outstanding educational opportunities are also afforded by attending international calligraphy conferences. Held annually since 1981, these conferences provide the calligraphic community with a forum for exchanging ideas and information through classes, exhibits and lectures.

Lettering can be functional, decorative, expressive and exciting. Handwritten letters can be used to write an entire text, as the focal point of a piece, or for personalization. Well-executed letters enhance any design; formal or informal, contemporary or traditional. While artists select styles and layouts appropriate to the content of the text, they must also devise solutions that work within the given limitations of their projects, such as size, cost and time.

Letters can be written directly with a pen, brush and a wide variety of suitable tools, or they can be drawn, constructed and retouched. Many lettering artists work with widely differing styles, while others prefer to specialize. Some create one-of-a-kind pieces, others concentrate on designing work for reproduction.

Calligraphy is a visual language all its own. The letters of the alphabet are more than just symbols for sounds; their individual shapes hold unlimited potential for artistic expression. To the viewer, even letters in a foreign language can be enticing. Designing with letterforms means not only having an intrinsic understanding of their structures and shapes, but also being able to arrange them effectively, taking into consideration composition, movement, rhythm and beauty. Not all pieces are intended to be beautiful; they can be powerful, striking or even disturbing depending on the artist's intent. A unique aspect of calligraphic art is that letterforms can serve as both the medium and the subject matter.

Some calligraphers give serious thought to the text, selecting lettering styles and layouts that visually enhance the meaning of the words. They often consider themselves vehicles for interpreting an author's work, and try to convey not only the author's intent, but their own reactions to it. Other calligraphic artists are motivated by the desire to create a design rich with texture and color. These artists find that calligraphic marks can excite and stimulate the eye and carry a message without requiring total legibility.

Calligraphers have become more adventurous in the last decade by exploring the use of unusual tools, methods and techniques, and experimenting with color, design and letterforms. In the tradition of the Abstract and Expressionist schools of painting, calligraphic artists have also developed a body of modern, expressive work. Much of the work of famed German lettering artists such as Ernst Schneidler, Karlgeorg Hoefer, Frederic Poppl and Rudolf Koch, is an outgrowth of the Expressionist movement. In America, Thomas Ingmire, Dick Beasley, and others pioneered a similar movement with their calligraphic paintings, crossing the boundaries between lettering and fine art. The innovative work of Charles Pearce, David Howells, Ann Hechle and a host of other contemporary artists has influenced a new generation of calligraphers worldwide.

Lettering Arts is organized in four parts. The first, "Alphabets," highlights creative interpretations of the Roman alphabet. "Commercial Lettering" presents lettering for reproduction such as that used on book jackets, and in logos, advertising and packaging. "Calligraphic Art" presents some extraordinary examples of lettering as an art form, and "Select Lettering Arts" features some of the best work published in *Calligraphy Review*, the foremost journal dedicated to calligraphic arts worldwide.

ALPHABET DESIGNS

From the world's greatest literature to yesterday's shopping list, a unique set of characters—an alphabet—is used as the basis of written communication in all languages. To calligraphers, the alphabet is more than a means of expressing ideas in words. It is a collection of letters whose beautiful shapes delight their vision and excite their creativity. Calligraphers share a joy in letterforms and the art they inspire.

An alphabet provides a perfect opportunity for exploring a myriad of design possibilities while unrestricted by the need to interpret a text. Each of the examples in this chapter treats the 26 letters of the Roman alphabet in a unique manner. From formal to funky, flourished to unadorned, elegant to casual, these alphabet designs have been created using a broad spectrum of tools, materials and styles.

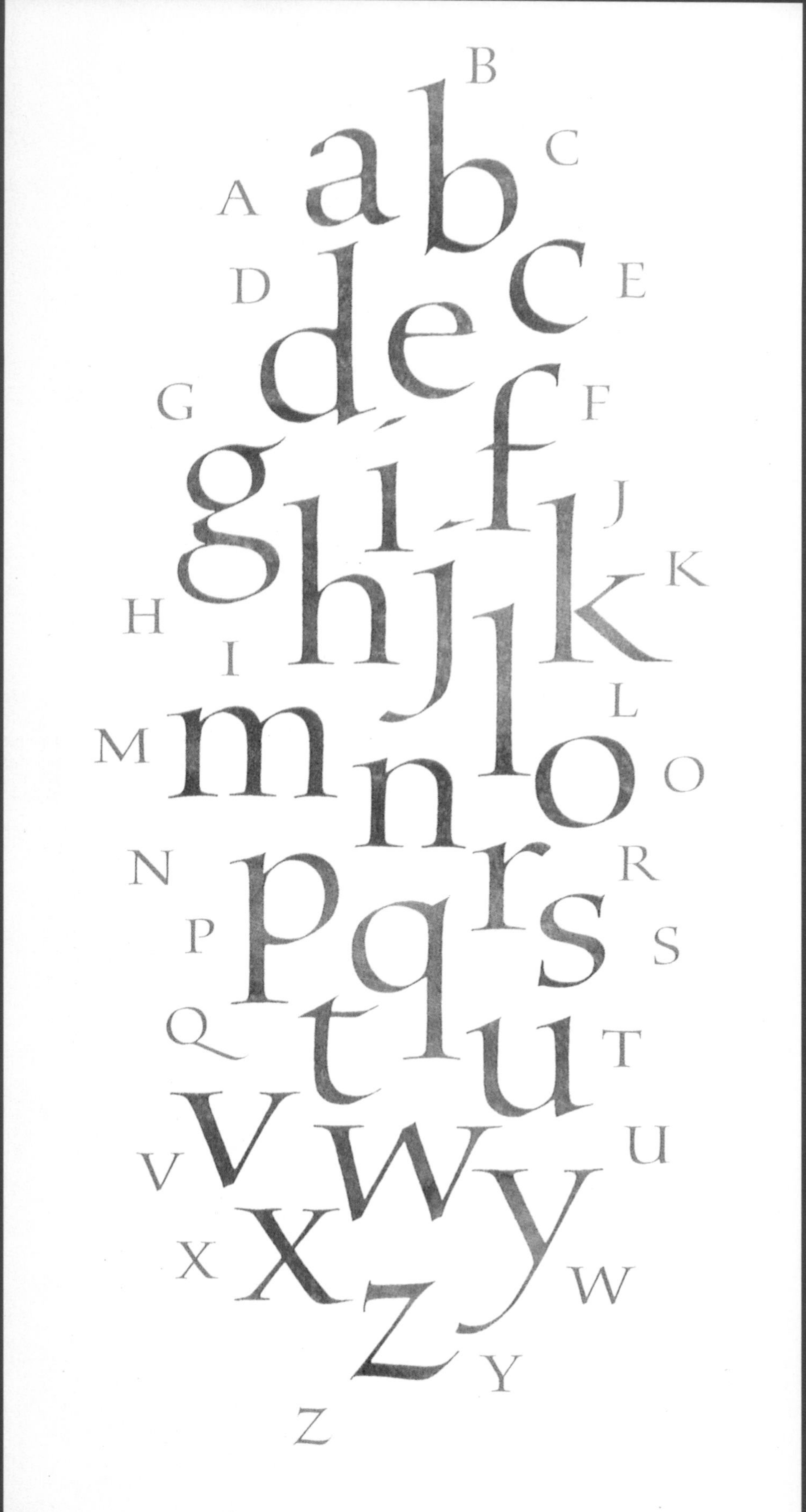
abcdefghijklmnopqrstuvwxyz
ABCDEFGHIJKLMNOPQRSTUVWXYZ

1

3

2

T COMME TERRE

1

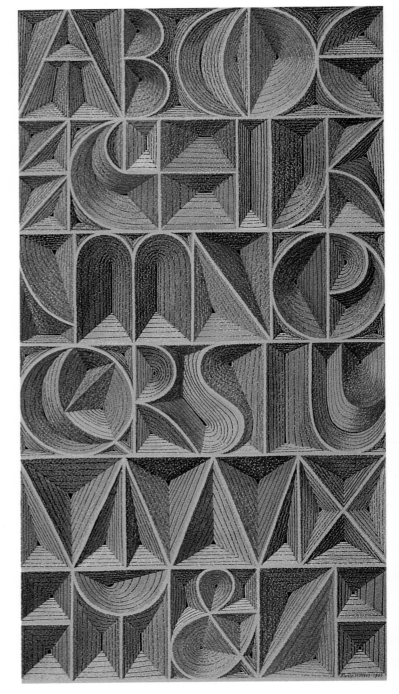

2

1
Myrna P. Rosen. *Untitled Alphabet*, 1986. 13 x 24. Speedball B nib, gouache, on Invicta parchment paper. Appeared in *Calligraphy Review*, Vol. 8, #2, Winter 1990.
2
Sheila Waters. *Alphabet in Three Dimensions, #1*, 1986. 9 x 18. Gouache, oil pastel and black Chinese stick ink on handmade watercolor paper. Photographed by Peter Waters. A variation of this piece appeared in *Calligraphy Review 1988 Annual*.
3-5
Rick Cusick. *Alphabet Complex*, 1990. 15 x 25. Ink, gouache, graphite and colored pencil.

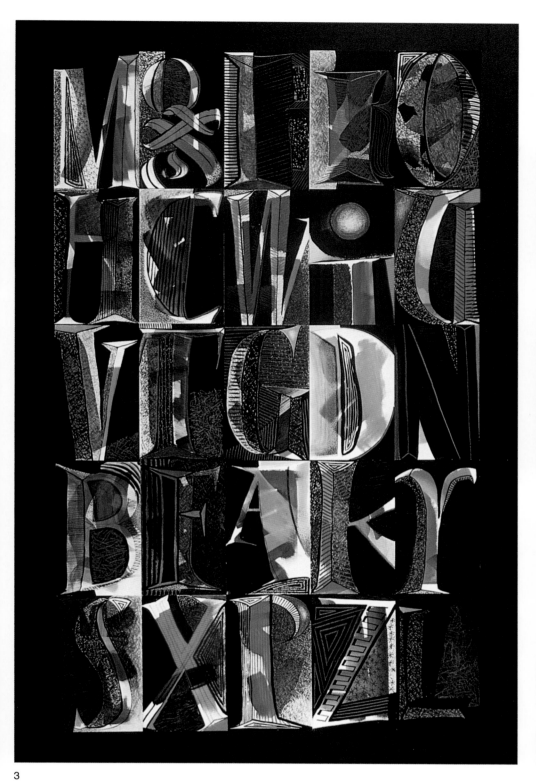

3

4

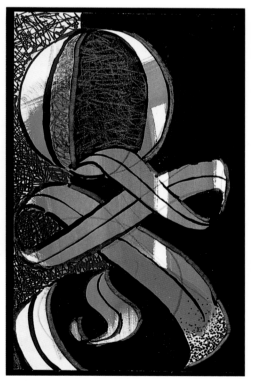

5

1

2

1
Peg Carlson. *Untitled*, 1992. 9 x 7. Brush and ink alphabet cut out and spray mounted on black gloss stock, gouache and neon tapes added.
2
Cheryl O. Adams. *Alphabet Design*, 1992. 3½ x 6. Designed and drawn by hand, then carved out of erasers and stamped.
3
Janell K. Wimberly. *Decorated Alphabet*, 1992. 25½ x 38. Mitchell nibs, brush, gouache, Luma pearlescent gold ink, on Strathmore black Grandee 65 lb. stock.

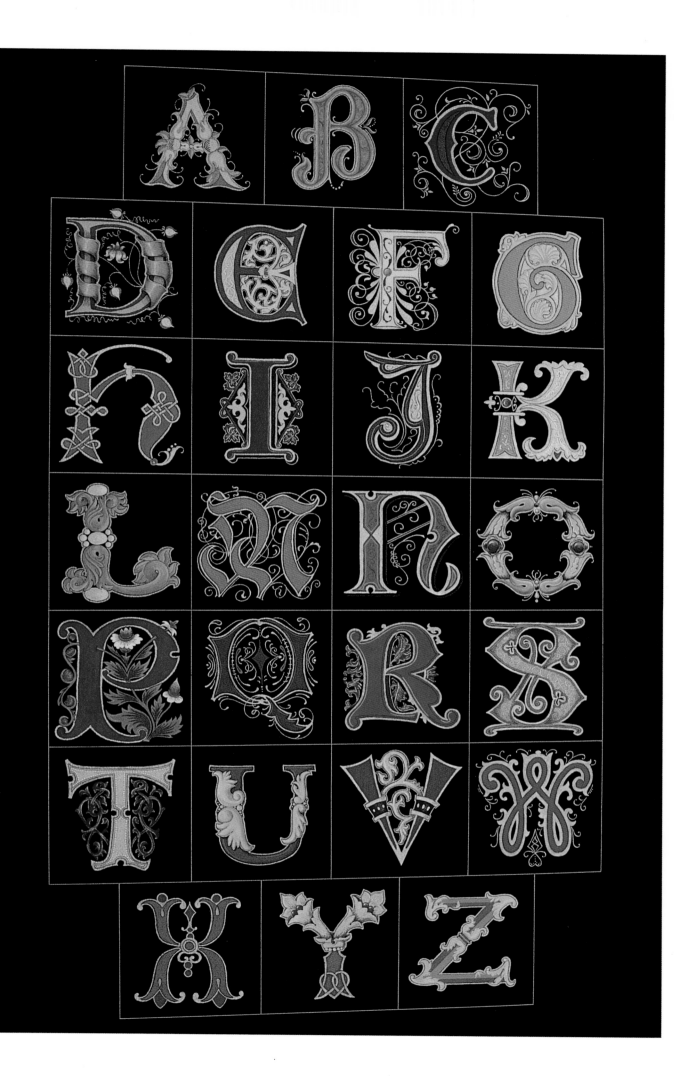

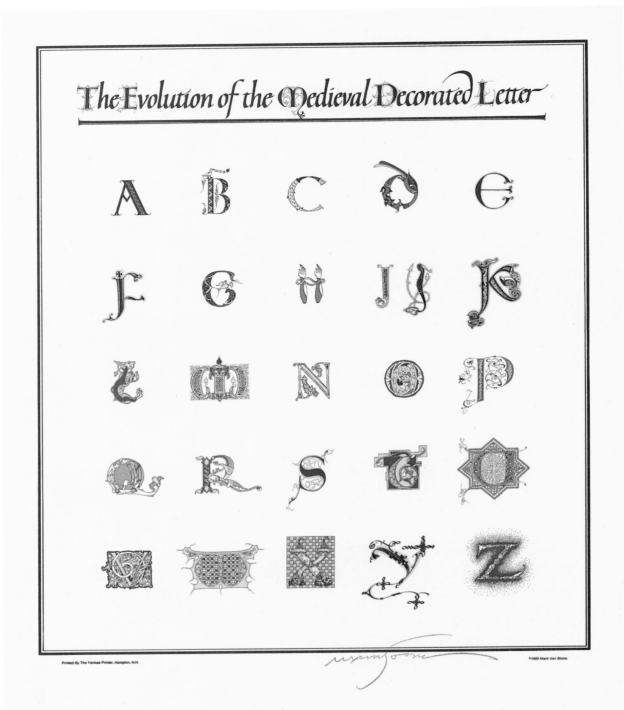

The Evolution of the Medieval Decorated Letter

3

1-3
Mark Van Stone. *Development of the Medieval Decorated Letter*, 1985. 18 x 22. Black ink on tracing paper. Printed from hand-color-separated artwork.
4
Alice Scott-Morris. *Alice's Alphabet*, 1991. 10 x 18. Rapidograph on drawing paper, photo etched into metal plates, printed on printmaking paper, hand colored with brush and watercolor.

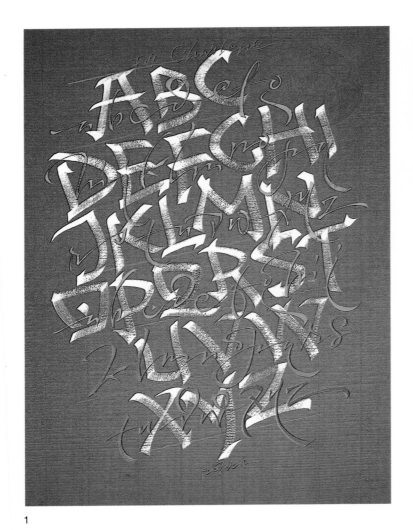

1

2

3

1-2
Carl Rohrs. *Alphabet*, 1989. Flat and pointed brushes, colored pencil, gouache on Roma paper. Photographed by Bill Reynolds.
3
Judy Kastin. *Alphabet*, 1992. 11 x 14. Pentel Color Brush, Rotring inks, sponge, on Strathmore 300 lb. cold press watercolor paper.
4
Mark Van Stone. *Variations on a Theme by Rudolf Koch*, 1992. 22 x 28. Ink on paper; offset printed.
5
Karlgeorg Hoefer. *UNCIAL-ABC-gespiegelt*, 1992. 48.5 cm. x 65.5 cm. Flat brush, 2 colors, gouache.

ZYXWVUTS
ZYXWVUTSRQPONMLKJIHGFEEDCB&A
RQPONM
ZYXWVUTSRQPONMLKJIHGFEEDCB&A
LKJIHGFE
ZYXWVUTSRQPONMLKJIHGFEEDCB&A
EDDCB&A

VARIATIONS ON A THEME BY RUDOLF KOCH
Mark Van Stone · 3422 Southeast Grant Court · Portland · Oregon · 97214 · USA
503 · 235 · 4035   fax 503 · 232 · 9256
letter design & historical ornament

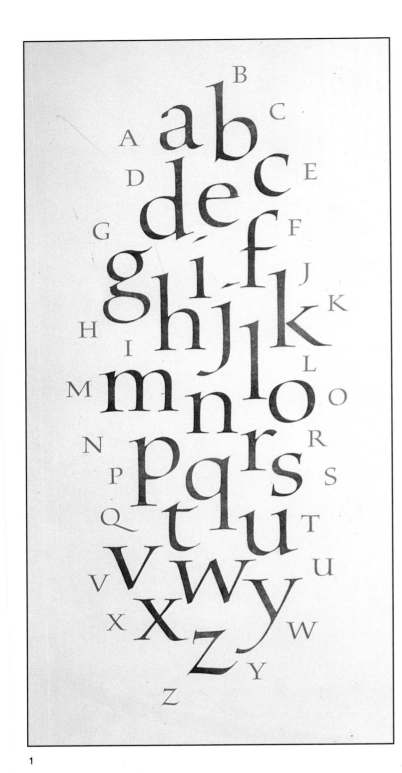

1

2

Aa Bb Cc
Dd Ee Ff Gg
Hh Ii Jj Kk
Ll Mm Nn Oo
Pp Qg Rr Ss
Tt Uu Vv Ww
Xx Yy Zz

3

4

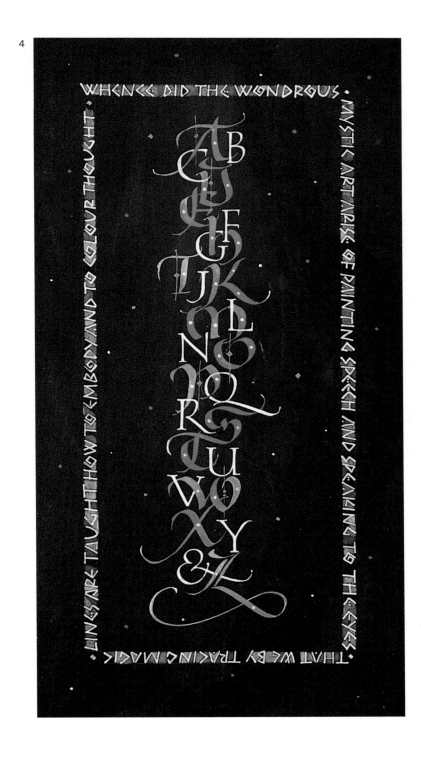

1

1-2
Tom Perkins. *Alphabet Design*, 1988. 7 x 16½. Welsh slate, letters incised with a mallet and chisel and painted off-white. Photographed by Frank Bird. Appeared in *Calligraphy Review l989 Annual*.

3
Gail Vick. *Display Alphabet; Anorexic, Lightweight*, 1990. 17 x 14. Pointed and edged nibs, black ink, white-out.

2

A B C D E F G H
I J K L M N O P
Q R S T U V W
X Y Z   G E E

3

Q

COMMERCIAL
LETTERING

Calligraphy and hand lettering began to have a major
impact on the graphic design industry in the early 1970s, when
Tim Girvin and other designers promoted the use of colorful,
exuberant lettering in combination with typography. By the
early 1980s, a number of talented calligraphers were specializing
in lettering for the commercial market. Prominent among them,
Georgia Deaver, John Stevens and Julian Waters are widely rec-
ognized for their impressive contributions. Today, dynamic
hand-lettered forms grace a variety of media and products.

Recent advances in computer technology have created incredi-
ble changes in the graphics industry. By the early 1990s, many
firms that had previously relied on artists' handwork turned to
computers to solve both their lettering and design problems.
Although some lettering artists use computers as design tools to
alter and enhance letterforms, computers cannot replace the
human hand; the spontaneity of the interaction when ink touches
paper can never be duplicated with bits and bytes.

Lettering designed for commercial purposes needs to entice the
consumer and to communicate a message. Most often commercial lettering requires legibility in a variety of sizes, from small
printed matter to lettering on giant billboards. When prepared
for reproduction, letters are often retouched and refined while
maintaining the freedom and flow of the original strokes.

DREAM SONG

Laura Lattig

David Scott Meier

1

2

3

1
Jean Formo. *Spectrum*, 1991. Mitchell nibs, technical pens, pencil, and stick inks. Client: Colleagues of Calligraphy.
2
John Stevens. *Pure Allure*, 1991. 8½ x 2⅞. Brushes, Sumi ink, on plate finish bristol board. Client: *Ladies Home Journal.* Art Director: Elsee Alpart.
3
Ludo Devaux. *Restaurant Logo*, 1990. 22 cm. x 3 cm. Felt tip pen.
4
Jane Dill. *Caritas*, 1992. 9 x 10½. Pens, quills and brushes, gouache, ink, and watercolor on watercolor paper. Client: American Heart Association. Art Director and Photographer: Bill Zemanek.

1

1
John Stevens. *Home Furnishing*, 1989. 3⅛ x 5½. Broad-edged nib, technical pens. Illustration: John Stevens. Client: Erin Edwards Advertising. Art Director: Ed Brennan.
2
John Stevens. *7 up*, 1989. 3½ x 4⅛. Broad-edged nib, brush, Sumi ink, on rice paper. Client: Shared Medical Systems.
3
John Stevens. *Voices of the Earth*, 1990. 4 x 4. Broad-edged nib, on bond paper. Client: Vital Body Marketing. Art Director: Bonnie Butler.
4
John Stevens. *Maverick*, 1991. Broad-edged nib and brush, on plate finish bristol board. Client: Maverick Design.
5
Anne V. Mackechnie. *Sinbad the Voyager*, 1990. Mitchell nib and Higgins Eternal ink. Client: March of Dimes.
6
Lawrence Brady. *International Letter Arts Network*, 1988. Brause nibs and stick ink on Arches cold press watercolor paper. Client: International Letter Arts Network.

2

3

4

5

6

1 Time to Blossom Out

2 ARTAGE

3 MONKEY CLUB

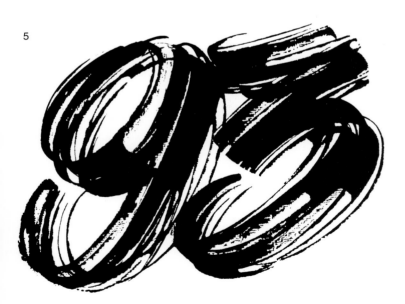

1
Henry Margulies. *Time to Blossom Out*, 1989. #170 Gillott nib on 2-ply kid finish Strathmore bristol board. Client: *Parents* magazine.
2
Jane Dill. *Artage*, 1992. 3 x 1½. Brush on watercolor paper. Client: Landor & Associates, San Francisco, CA. Art Director: Elizabeth Shoemaker.
3
Jill Bell. *Monkey Club*, 1988. 7 x 1½. Pen and ink. Client: A & R Advertising / Monkey Club.
4
Henry Margulies. *Numerals 1,2,3,4,5,6,7,8,9,0*, 1990. #850 Gillott nib, on 2-ply kid finish Strathmore bristol board. Client: Saks Fifth Avenue. Art Director: Ross Bonanno.
5
Jean Larcher. *93*, 1992. 24 cm. x 32 cm. Pentel Color Brush, ruling pen, black India ink on MBM Ingres d'Arches paper. Client: Fédération des Foires & Salons de France. Art Director: Marylène Vanvam Kides.

1

Calligraphy

AT

STEUBEN

2

The National Symphony Orchestra Ball 1990

3

4

1
Patricia Weisberg. *Calligraphy at Steuben*, 1992. Speedball nib, ink, on bond paper. Silkscreened on shop glass facade. Client: Steuben Glass.
2
Julian Waters. *National Symphony Orchestra*, 1990. Broad-edged nib and ink. Client: National Symphony Orchestra.
3-4
Georgia Deaver. *Volunteers: A Symphony of Service Poster*, 1991. Brush, broad-edged nib, watercolor, and gouache on handmade paper. Client: © California Association of Hospitals and Health Systems. Art Director: Linda Clark Johnson, Marketing by Design.

1

1-2
Dick Beasley. *The Arboretum at Flagstaff*, 1992. Client: Judy and Wayne
Hite, Arboretum at Flagstaff.
3
Julian Waters. *A.A.R.P. "Purposes" Poster*, 1988. Pen and ink. Client:
American Association of Retired Persons. Art Director: Bill Caldwell.

2

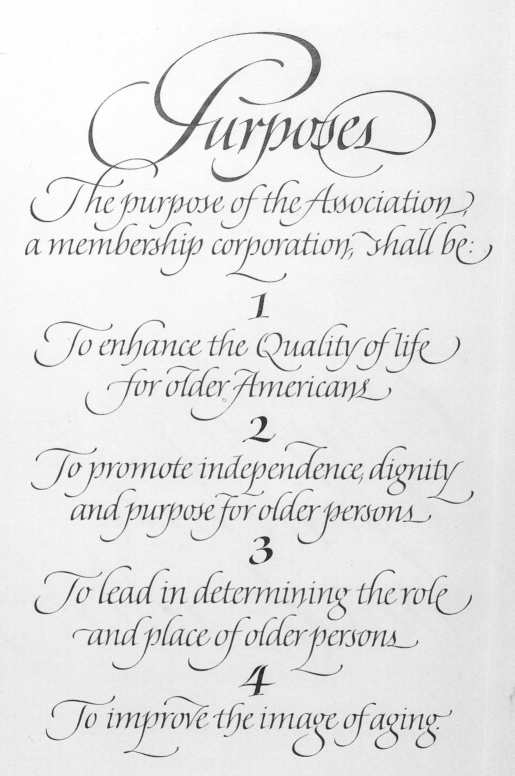

Purposes

The purpose of the Association, a membership corporation, shall be:

1
To enhance the Quality of life for older Americans

2
To promote independence, dignity and purpose for older persons

3
To lead in determining the role and place of older persons

4
To improve the image of aging.

AMERICAN ASSOCIATION OF RETIRED PERSONS

Article 1, Section 2. Bylaws of the American Association of Retired Persons

1

Thank you

2

Compagnie Générale des Eaux

3

Greater Pittsburgh

4

A Two for One
Challenge

The alumni/ae of PSR are
challenged in a new way!

Several alumni/ae
have offered a total of
$15,000 in matching gifts
to encourage new support
from you, the people who
have benefited the most
from the School.

The first alumni/ae I will
be introducing to you on
behalf of the Alumni/ae
Council who have made
this challenge possible
are Judy and Ed Hoerr
of Peoria, Illinois. I think
their letter of witness and
support speaks for itself,
so let me explain how
the challenge works.

For every $2.00 you con-
tribute to PSR's 1983-84
Annual Fund, the Hoerrs
and other alumni/ae will
give $1.00. If the alumni/ae
give an additional $30,000
we will raise $45,000 for
the needs of the future
ministers who are today's
PSR students.

These students need
adequate financial aid.
They need a faculty
supported and enriched
during their teaching tenure
and well-maintained
housing and classrooms.
Without this support, who
will replace the alumni/ae
in future ministries?

Give now! Double what you
gave last year to ensure
this two for one match.

If you have not given
through the Alumni/ae
Fund in the past, this is
a good year to begin.

Thank you for your
support!

Charlotte Russell '72
Alumni/ae Council
President

1
Claude Dieterich A. *Thank You*, 1990. 5 x 4. Pointed pen, stick ink, on
drawing paper. Client: Key Graphics, Key Biscayne, FL.
2
Jean Larcher. *Compagnie Générale des Eaux*, 1992. 30 cm. x 50 cm.
Black India ink, X-acto knife, French curves, on scratchboard. Client:
EDIFI Agency. Art Director: Catherine Duthoit.
3
Paul P. Herrera. *Greater Pittsburgh*, 1991. 10½ x 2½. Rapidograph pen,
red sable pointed brush, Higgins Eternal black, F/W ink, on Bienfang paper.
Client: Waterway Collection. Art Director: Michael F. Blaser.
4
Georgia Deaver. *Pacific School of Religion Brochure*, 1983. 9 x 15½.
Broad-edged pen on watercolor paper. Client: © Pacific School of Religion.
Art Director: Michael Mabry, Michael Mabry Design.

1
Brenda Walton. *A Beautiful Tradition*, 1992. 9¼ x 11. Technical pens on drafting vellum. Client: Liberty House, Hawaii. Art Director: Kathy Nunokawa, Liberty House Advertising.
2
Dick Beasley. *Flagstaff Symphony Orchestra Bravo 40th Season Program Cover*, 1989. 6 x 9. FW colored inks, white gouache on layout bond paper. Client: Harold Weller, Conductor, Flagstaff Symphony Orchestra.
3-4
Iskra Johnson. *Winter Concerto*, 1990. Closed, 3⅝ x 5½. Open, 14¾ x 5½. Text, Mitchell pens; "Joy," pointed brush on bond paper; background, brush on cover text. Marbled paper modified on photocopier for borders and backgrounds. Author/composer: Vivaldi.

WINTER

concerto

· L'INVERNO · · VIVALDI ·

Frozen and shivering in the icy snow,
Agghiacciato tremor tra nevi algenti

In the strong blasts of a terrible wind;
Al severo spirar d'orrido Vento,

To run stamping one's feet at every step,
Correr battendo i piedi ogni momento,

With one's teeth chattering through the cold;
E pel soverchio gel batter i denti;

To spend the quiet & happy days by the fire,
Passar al foco i dì quieti e contenti

Whilst outside the rain soaks everyone;
Mentre la pioggia fuor bagna ben cento.

To walk on the ice with slow steps,
Caminar sopra 'l ghiaccio e a passo lento

And go carefully for fear of falling:
Per timor di cader girsene intenti:

To go in haste, slide and fall down,
Gir forte, sdrucciolar, cader a terra

To go again on the ice and run,
Di nuovo ir sopra 'l ghiaccio e corer forte

Until the ice cracks and opens;
Sin che 'l ghiaccio si rompe, e si disserra;

To hear leaving their iron-gated houses,
Sentir uscir dalle ferrate porte

Scirocco, Boreas and all the winds in battle;
Scirocco, Borea e tutti i Venti in guerra.

Sonnet to „Le Quattro Stagione", Concerto No. 4

Seasons Greetings from
Iskra Lettering Design

Calligraphy
& Design
by Iskra

This is Winter but it brings *Joy*

1-3
Alice. *Society of Scribes, Ltd.* 15th Anniversary, 1989. 14 x 17. Speedball
C-series nib, Fount India ink, 2-ply Strathmore vellum paper. Client:
Society of Scribes, Ltd. Banner painted by Will Farrington.

1

2

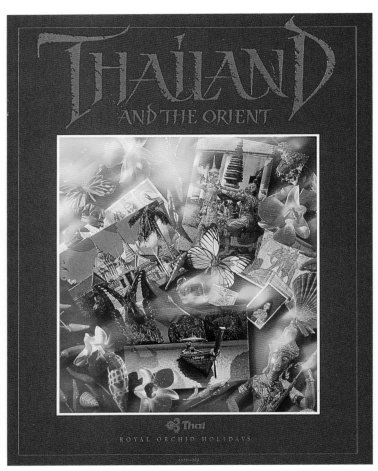

3

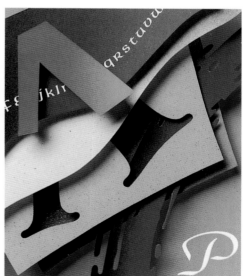

5

1

Brenda Walton. *Contadina Labels*, 1988. 3½ diameter. Original: 5 x 2¼.
Pointed sable brush, Pelikan Fount India ink on dull coated stock. Client:
Contadina. Art Director: Thomas Bond, SBG Partners, San Francisco, CA.

2

Georgia Deaver. Cento per Cento Wine Label, 1992. 4⅝ x 3¹⁵⁄₁₆. Broad-
edged pen on drafting vellum. Client: © Viansa Winery, Sam Sebastianni.
Art Director: Patti Britton, Britton Design.

3

Iskra Johnson. *Thai Airlines*, 1991. Automatic pen, Pelikan 4001 ink on cold
press watercolor paper. Client: Thai Airlines. Art Director: David Vostmeyer.
Photographed by Tom Collicott.

4-5

Nancy Stentz. *Hewlett Packard Scalable Typeface Disk Collection Jackets*,
1990. 15¼ x 9¼. Art Director: Mary Gogulski, Floathe Johnson Associates.

1

2

1
Lennart Hansson. *Rystadius*, 1983. Client: Rystadius Auktioner.
2
Lennart Hansson. *SOS*, 1980. Client: SOS AB.
3
Lennart Hansson. *Café Nouveau*, 1988. Client: Café Nouveau Restaurant, Falun, Sweden.
4
Lennart Hansson. *Insikt (Insight)*, 1991. Client: Alf AB, Malmö, Sweden.

3

4

1

Amore

2

Amore

3

THANK YOU

4

1-2
Jane Dill. *Amore*, 1992. 9 x 2¾. Brush on paper towel. Client: Amore
Publications, Inc., New York, NY. Art Directors: Jane Dill, Jennie Hansen.
3
Mary Lou O'Brian. *Thank You*, 1987. 6 x 4. Felt tip brush marker on
Indian paper.
4
Patricia Weisberg. *Blue J*, 1990. 8¼ x 7⅜. "J" drawn and inked with brush,
"Blue" in marker, bird's feathered crown with Speedball nib and ink. Client:
The Michigan Association of Calligraphers, Mohawk Paper Mills, and the
Michigan Council for the Arts. Art Director: Susan Skarsgard.

1-2
Patricia Weisberg. *Hi*, 1992. 4¼ x 5½. Pen, ink, colored markers, bond paper. Photocopied and hand colored.
3-4
Georgia Deaver. *Greeting Cards*, 1986. 5 x 7. Brushes and broad-edged nibs. Client: © Neugebauer Verlag, Salzburg, Austria.
5
Paul Shaw. *1989 New Year's Card*, 1988. 7 x 10. Ruling pen on Bienfang Graphics 36 paper with Higgins Engrossing ink; printed letterpress on Japanese paper in reverse on back side (numbers show through) for white 1-7; printed on front in coffee color; numbers '89 and pink type Gill Sans Light, Monotype; printed by Peter Kruty.

1

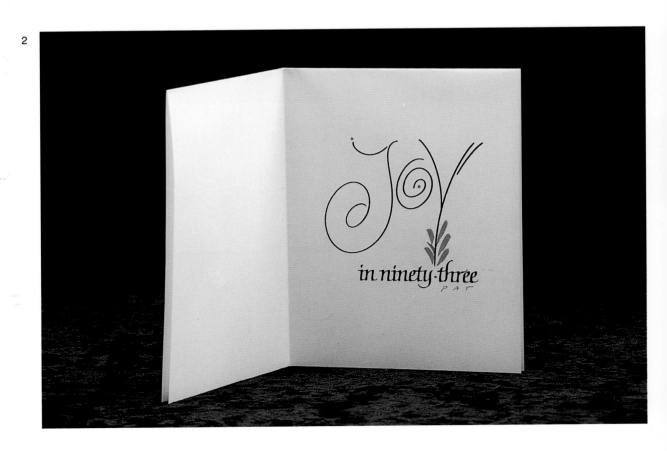

2

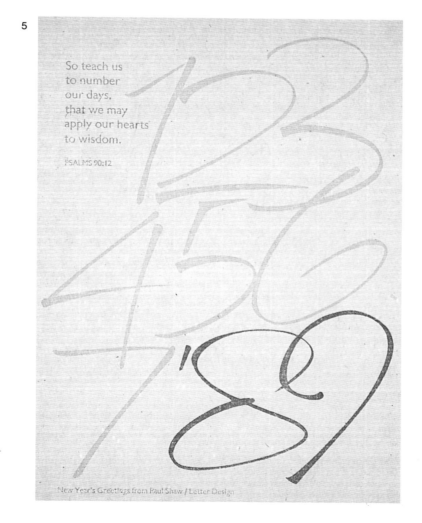

So teach us
to number
our days,
that we may
apply our hearts
to wisdom.

PSALMS 90:12

New Year's Greetings from Paul Shaw / Letter Design

ON THE FIRST DAY
OF CHRISTMAS
MY TRUE LOVE SENT
TO ME

A partridge in a pear tree.

Mr. and Mrs. Gilbert M. Fried request the honour of your presence at

GLADNESS
LOVE
JOY

the marriage of
their daughter   Liane

to   Dr. Joel
Steven Adler   son of
Mr. and Mrs. Melvin Adler

MARRIAGE

on Sunday, the 19th of November, Nineteen hundred and eighty-nine at twelve o'clock
at the Crystal Plaza, 305 West Northfield Road, Livingston, New Jersey
Reception to follow ceremony   R.S.V.P.

HAPPY
HOLIDAYS

1

1
Georgia Deaver. *Partridge in a Pear Tree Christmas Card*, 1991. Closed, 4⅜ x 5½ Open, 13⅛ x 5½. Brush and broad-edged pen. Printed in black on Wyndstone paper, hand colored with pastels.
2
Paul Shaw. *Wedding Announcement*, 1989. 8 x 8. Original: Brause nibs, Higgins India ink on vellum bristol board and Arches watercolor paper. Printed letterpress on Japanese paper by Peter Kruty. Client: Liane Fried.
3
Ward Dunham & Linnea Lundquist. *Passion*, 1992. 7 x 5. Chinese ink on butcher paper. Letterpress printed on handmade Twinrocker paper.

3

1

1-2
Chris A. Paschke. *Wedding 91*, 1991. Closed, 5 x 7. Open, 10¼ x 10¼. Original: Brause nibs, Sumi ink on layout paper. Two-color offset print on handmade Indian watercolor paper. Gold notary seal with custom designed monogram transposed onto hand embosser. Author: James C. Lofink. Client: James C. Lofink.

3-4
Brenda Walton. *Robin & Steven*, 1989. 13¼ x 4½. Pencil on tracing paper, and type. Clients: Robin Rodness and Steven Zari. Art Director: Andrea Barkin, Pat Davis Design.

2

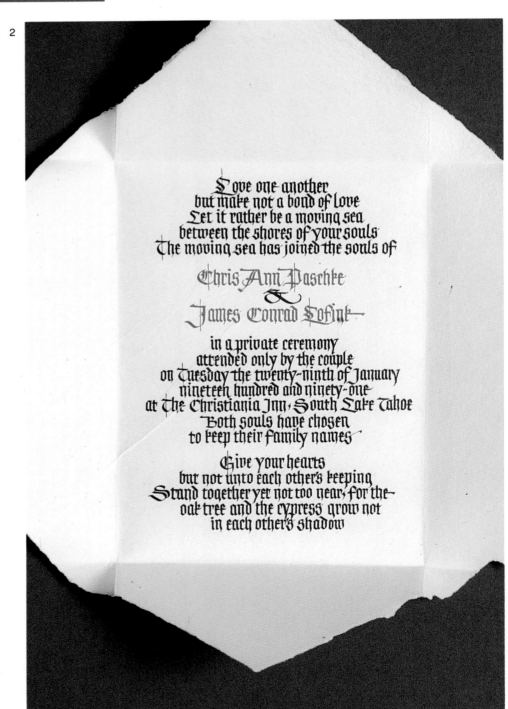

Love one another
but make not a bond of love
Let it rather be a moving sea
between the shores of your souls
The moving sea has joined the souls of

Chris Ann Paschke
&
James Conrad Lofink

in a private ceremony
attended only by the couple
on Tuesday the twenty-ninth of January
nineteen hundred and ninety-one
at The Christiania Inn, South Lake Tahoe
Both souls have chosen
to keep their family names

Give your hearts
but not unto each other's keeping
Stand together yet not too near, for the
oak tree and the cypress grow not
in each other's shadow

1

2

1-2
C.A. Millner. *P*, 1990. Blue Pumpkin nib, Chinese stick ink, technical pens on Strathmore 13 lb. layout bond.

3
C.A. Millner. *Holiday Card - Noel*, 1990. Blue Pumpkin nib, Chinese stick ink, technical pens on Strathmore 13 lb. layout bond.

4
Paul Shaw. *Episcopal Church Christmas Card*, 1990. 5 x 7. Brause pens on vellum bristol board with Higgins India ink; letters (and illustrations) then cut in wood by David Frampton and printed on Japanese paper in 4 colors; PMS colors offset printed on Mohawk Superfine paper. Client: Episcopal Church. Art Director: Rochelle Arthur.

5
Michael W. Hughey. *Branch of Peace*, 1989. 5 x 7. Brushes, colored markers, watercolor and gouache on paper. Client: Twin Dolphin Press. © Michael W. Hughey.

3

ALL THIS WE COULD BEAR IF WE KNEW WE DID NOT SUFFER IN VAIN; THAT GOD WAS BESIDE US · IN THE STRUGGLE, SHARING THE MISERIES OF HIS OWN WORLD · FOR THE RIDDLE OF THE WORLD IS THIS: SHALL SORROW AND LOVE BE RECONCILED AT LAST, WHEN THE PROMISED KINGDOM COMES?

4

5

1

1
Holly Sanford Faulk. *Get Well Soon*, 1992. Cut-outs from magazines, photographs, etc.
2
Georgia Deaver. *Happy Chanukah Card*, 1988. 5 x 7. Brush and broad-edged nib. Client: © Marcel Schurman. Art Director: Sandra MacMillan.
3
Joanne Fink. *Love is Sharing*, 1990. 14 x 18. Tape nib, Rexel nib, Holbein gouache, Higgins Eternal ink on Strathmore bristol board. Author: Joanne Fink.
4
Joanne Fink. *Initials*, 1992. 9 x 12. Powell pen, Holbein gouache on Strathmore vellum surface bristol board.

2

LOVE IS SHARING ALL THE WONDERFUL THINGS LIFE HAS TO OFFER WITH THE PERSON YOU CARE MOST ABOUT ANYTHING IS POSSIBLE IF YOU DO IT TOGETHER

By sharing your hopes and thoughts and dreams, your love will flourish. Work with each other to build your lives together and you will grow in love. May your lives be forever intertwined, your love always bringing you closer. May you create a home that expresses your individuality and your love for one another. May it be a home filled with peace, with happiness, and especially with love.

3

4

1

Glen Epstein 1993 Calendar of Country Knowledge & Extraordinary Americana

2

July

3

August

1-3
Julian Waters. *Glen Epstein's Calendar*, 1992. Pen and ink. Client: Glen Epstein.
4
Julian Waters. *Audubon Calendar*, 1990. Client: Macmillan Publishing Co. Art Director: Janet Tingey.
5-6
Julian Waters. *Relationships Calendar*, 1990. Powell brass pen, ink. Client: S & S Graphics, Inc. Art Director: Tony Fitch. Photographed by Gary Landsman. Appeared in *Calligraphy Review 1990 Annual*.

4

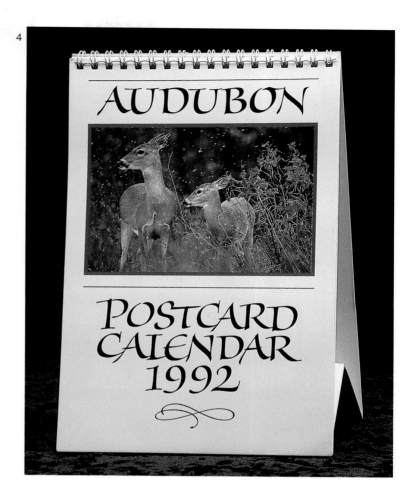

5

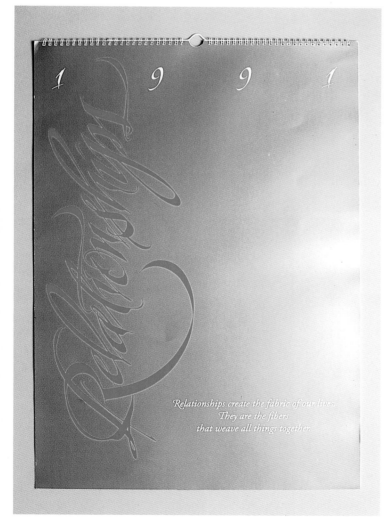

6

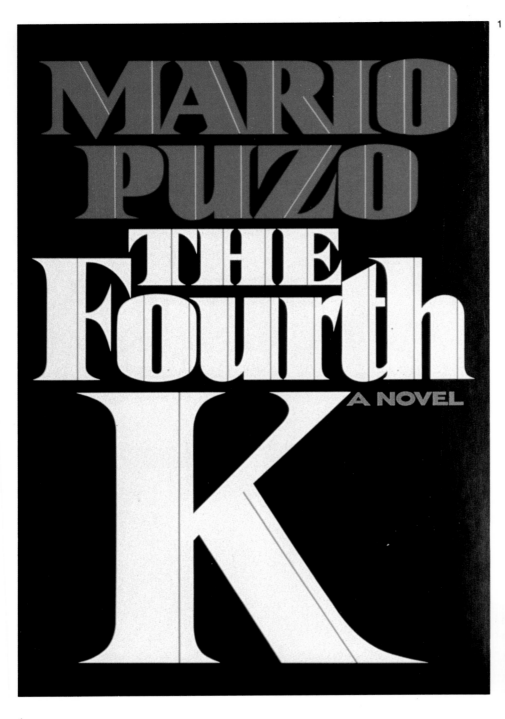

1
David Gatti. *The Fourth K*, 1990. 6¼ x 9½. Pen and brush, ink on bristol board. Author: Mario Puzo. Client: Random House. Art Director: Robert Aulicino.
2
David Gatti. *The Sands of Time*, 1989. 6¼ x 9⁷⁄₁₆. Pen and brush, ink on bristol board. Author: Sidney Sheldon. Client: William Morrow & Company, Inc. Art Director: Cheryl Asherman.
3
Iskra Johnson. *Imajica*, 1991. Chisel-edged brush, gouache. Retouched on photostat with brush and technical pen. Author: Clive Barker. Client: HarperCollins. Art Director: Gene Mydlowski. Illustrated by Kirk Reinert.

BESTSELLING AUTHOR OF THE GREAT AND SECRET SHOW

CLIVE BARKER

IMAJICA

1
Julian Waters. *Dream Song*. Speedball C nib, ink. Client: Picture Book Studio.
Author: Laura Lattig. Art Director: Robert Saunders. Illustrated by
David Scott Meier.
2
Anthony Bloch. *The Ultimate Dinosaur*, 1992. 25¾ x 11⅛. Brause nib on
Hammermill ledger bond, touched up and antiqued with white-out. Authors:
Philip Currie, Ray Bradbury, Peter Dodson, Harry Harrison, Gregory Benford,
Sankar Chatterjee. Client: Byron Preiss Visuals. Art Director: Dean Motler.
3
Julian Waters. *The Speedball Textbook, 22nd Edition*, 1991. 5¾ x 8½.
Lettering done with Mitchell nibs and Chinese stick ink on Norwegian layout
bond paper. Background wash by Joanne Fink done with Holbein gouache
and Winsor & Newton 580 series brush. Client: Hunt Manufacturing Co.

1

2

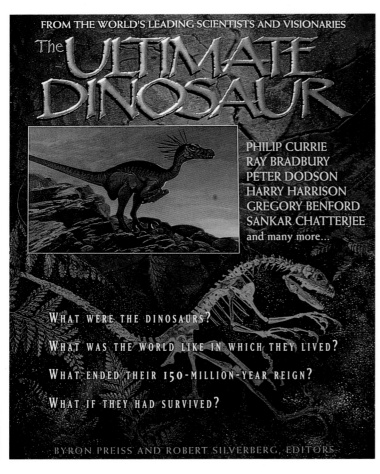

The Speedball® Textbook

22ND EDITION   A COMPREHENSIVE GUIDE TO PEN AND BRUSH LETTERING

Good Morning Good Night

Ivan Gantschev

1

SIMON AND THE HOLY NIGHT

Eve Tharlet

2

1
Julian Waters. *Good Morning, Good Night*, 1991. Speedball nib, India ink, on bond paper. Author: Ivan Gantscher. Client: Picture Book Studio. Art Director: Robert Saunders. Illustrated by David DeRan.
2
Julian Waters. *Simon and the Holy Night*, 1991. Mitchell nib, Chinese stick ink, on layout bond paper. Author: Eve Tharlet. Client: Picture Book Studio. Art Director: Robert Saunders.

Lon Po Po

A RED-RIDING HOOD STORY FROM CHINA

ED YOUNG

MADELEINE L'ENGLE
The Glorious Impossible
ILLUSTRATED WITH FRESCOES FROM THE SCROVEGNI CHAPEL BY
GIOTTO

Wind in the Long Grass

The Tinderbox — Hans Christian Andersen — Illustrated by James Warhola

Dancing the Breeze — By George Shannon · Pictures by Jacqueline Rogers

JOHN STEPTOE
Mufaro's Beautiful Daughters
AN AFRICAN TALE

1
John Stevens. *Lon Po Po*, 1989. Chinese brush, broad-edged nib, Sumi ink on rice paper. Author: Ed Young. Client: Northrop. Art Director: Nanette Stevenson.
2
John Stevens. *The Glorious Impossible*, 1990. Broad-edged nibs. Author: Madeleine L'Engle. Client: Simon & Schuster. Art Director: Sylvia Frezzolini.
3
John Stevens. *Wind in the Long Grass*, 1991. Broad-edged nib, ink on paper. Author: William Higginson. Client: Simon & Schuster. Art Director: Vicki Kalajian. Illustrated by Sandra Speidel.
4
John Stevens. *The Tinderbox*, 1990. Broad-edged nibs, brush on bond paper. Client: Simon & Schuster. Art Director: Lucille Chomowitz.
5
John Stevens. *Dancing the Breeze*, 1990. Broad-edged nib on bond paper. Author: George Shannon. Client: Bradbury Press. Art Director: Julie Quon. Illustrated by Jacqueline Rogers.
6
John Stevens. *Mufaro's Beautiful Daughters*, 1986. Broad-edged nib. Author: John Steptoe. Art Director: Rachel Simon.

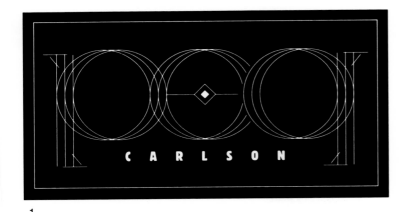

1

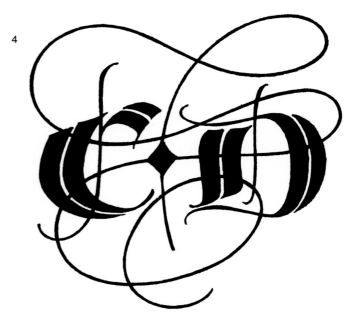

4

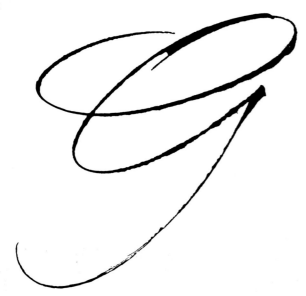

2

1
Rick Cusick. *Bookplate for Peg Carlson*, 1992. 1⅝ x 3. Designed on paper, finished on Macintosh computer. Client: Cheryl Jacobsen.
2
C.A. Millner. *G Monogram*, 1992. 4¼ x 5. Glass pen, liquid Sumi ink on Fabriano Italia paper. Client: Gregory Garritt.
3
Lynn Broide. *"Shemesh" (Sun)*. 3⅛ x 1⁹⁄₁₆. Speedball nib.
4
Mary Lou O'Brian. *Monogram "CD,"* 1992. 2¼ x 2¼. Drawn with a Rotring style fountain pen on Arches paper. Client: Christopher Drayton.
5-6
Julian Waters. *Wildflowers*, 1992. Pen and ink. Client: U.S. Postal Service. Art Director: Derry Noyes. Photographed by Hans Reinhard. Appeared in *Calligraphy Review 1991 Annual*.

3

Wildflowers

A Collection of
U.S. Commemorative Stamps

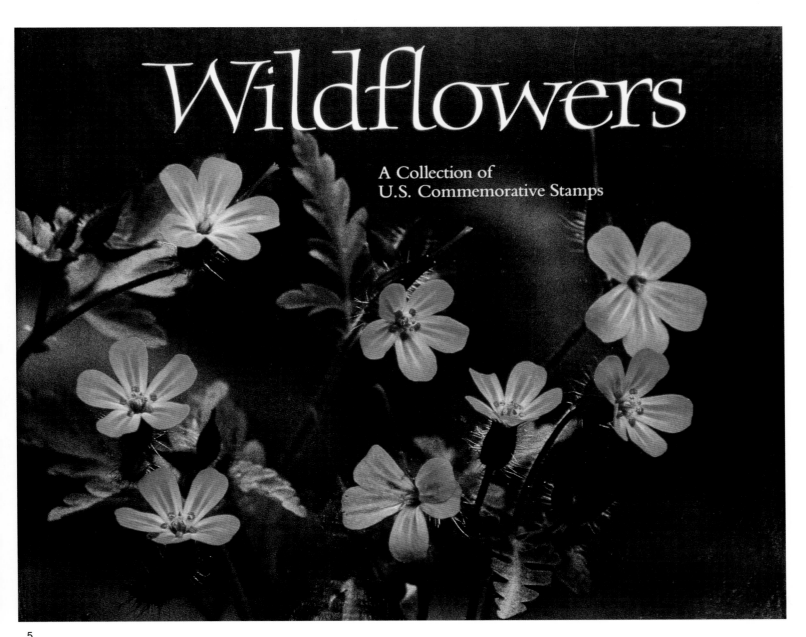

5

6 Rue Anemone

Fireweed

Meadow Beauty

Stream Violet

Jack-in-the-Pulpit

1
Cheryl O. Adams. *Squished*, 1991. 8¼ x 3⅝. Coit pen, ink on bond paper.
2
Iskra Johnson. *Near Dark*, 1987. 10 wide. Chisel-edged brush on Hammermill bond paper.
3
Iskra Johnson. *Zen*, 1992. 5 wide. Japanese brush, Pelikan Fount India ink on Teton text paper. Client: *Home* magazine. Art Director: Ragnar Johnsen.
4
Nancy Stentz. *Pulsations*, 1992. Design marker on textured paper. Client: Providence Hospital. Art Director: David McKeague.
5
Nancy Stentz. *Shoebop*, 1991. Client: Alexandria Rossoff.
6
Nancy Stentz. *The Number One Espresso*, 1991. Design marker on tracing paper. Client: Venettos Coffee Co. Art Director: Jim Ault Advertising Assoc.

4

Pulsations

5

Sho-Bop

6

The Number One Espresso

1

2

1
Anne V. Mackechnie. *Spooners*, 1990. Drawn letters filled in with black ink. Client: Spooners Ice Cream.
2
Nancy Stentz. *Godzillas.* Client: Wayne Palmer, P & P Distributors.
3
Anne V. Mackechnie. *Carved in Stone*, 1992. Technical pen, flat brush, natural sponge, white-out.
4
Brenda Walton. *Harbourfront Inn*, 1989. Original 4 x 3. Metal nib, Pelikan Fount India ink on Roma paper. Client: Harbourfront Inn. Art Director: Randy Borns, Borns Design, Grandhaven, MI.
5
Anne V. Mackechnie. *Will Lewis*, 1992. Drawn letters, amberlith overlay. Client: Will Lewis, RB Records.
6
Ludo Devaux. *Kalligrafie*, 1989. Poster 35 cm. x 4 cm. Automatic pen, gouache, handmade paper.

3

4

WILL LEWIS

KALLIGRAFIE

Bellefleur[1]

SAVILLE[2]

1
Nancy Stentz. *Bellefleur*, 1992. Client: John Culbertson. Art Director: Sebastian Titus.
2
Nancy Stentz. *Saville*, 1992. Technical pen, hot press illustration board. Client: Saville. Art Director: Matt Smith, Bon Marché Advertising.
3
Rick Cusick. *Lettering for Castles Calendar*, 1989. Client: © Hallmark Cards, Inc.
4
Martin Jackson. *Martin Jackson Ltd.*, 1988. 7⅞ x 3¼. Technical pen and brush on tracing paper.

3

4

Hacienda

1

2

HISPANIC CULTURAL ARTS

3

LATIN AMERICA

1
Iskra Johnson. *Hacienda*, 1992. 13 x 3¹⁄₁₆. Chisel brush, gouache on Teton
text paper. Client: Hacienda Resort & Convention Center. Art Director:
Earl Grizzell.
2
Claude Dieterich A. *Hispanic Cultural Arts*, 1989. 7 x 4. Flat brush, stick ink
on board. Client: Hispanic Cultural Arts, Fort Lauderdale, FL.
3
Claude Dieterich A.. *Latin America*, 1989. 6½ x 2½. Flat brush, stick ink on
board. Client: Ladatco, Miami, FL. Art Director: Mel Holland.
4
Brenda Walton. *Sailing the Harbor*, 1991. 16½ x 10½. Various materials.
Art Director: Mike Borosky, Cronan Design.

Wow! Congratulations

LOVE  Anniversary Wishes

The GREAT ACTS OF Love are done by those who habitually perform small acts of kindness.

I LOVE YOU

שלום

Happy Birthday!

Never forget THAT THE MOST POWERFUL FORCE ON EARTH IS Love.

Happy Anniversary

party

Season's Greetings

You're Invited

MERRY CHRISTMAS

1

1
Joanne Fink & Judy Kastin. *Lettering Brochure*, 1992. 8½ x 11. Various pens and brushes. Offset printed on coated stock.
Client: Calligrapher's Ink, Ltd.
2
Mary Lou O'Brian. *Shapes*, 1991. 7½ x 4. Felt tip brush marker on Musee paper. Client: Shapes Aerobics Program.
3
Iskra Johnson. *Chutzpah*, 1990. 7⅝ x 2½. Japanese brush, jet black gouache on Teton text paper.
4
Mary Lou O'Brian. *Sigma*, 1991. 7 x 3¼. Ruling pen and Sumi ink on Musee paper. Client: Sigma Corporation.
5
Cheryl Jacobsen. *Hawkeyes*, 1992. 7½ x 3. Pentel Color Brush on watercolor paper. Client: University of Iowa Women's Athletic Dept. Art Director: Patti O'Neil.

2 *Shapes*

3 *Chutzpah!*

4 *Sigma*

5 *Hawkeyes*

1

2

1
Mike Kecseg. *Mother Plate*, 1990. 8 diameter. Original: pointed pen and ink on paper. Author: B. J. Hoff. Client: Abbey Press. Art Director: C. J. Brown.

2
Leslie Gattman and Eugene Frank. *Wedding Goblets*. 3½ x 6¼. Porcelain with underglaze pencil, painted underglaze, clear overglaze, gold luster. Text: Old Testament, Song of Songs.

3
Chava Wolpert Richard. *Honey and Apple Plate*, 1981. 9½ diameter. Silkscreen on porcelain. English lettering: Lili Cassel Wronker.

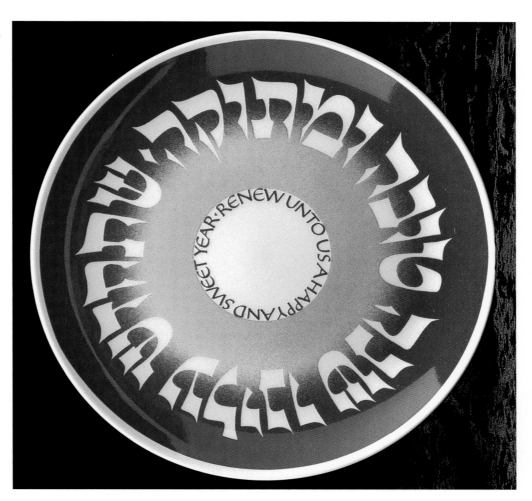

CALLIGRAPHIC ART

Calligraphy entered a new era when artists who were using letters as their medium began to produce pieces that went beyond function alone. Some create works of exquisite beauty, others move their viewers with powerful, provocative images. These boundary-breaking artists seek public recognition for their art.

Today calligraphic art runs the gamut from traditionally based pieces to modern expressive work. Not all lettering is intended to be read; calligraphic marks can make an exciting design with or without legible text. In a composition, artists may choose to make lettering the only feature, or combine it with other visual elements such as watercolor or collage images.

Although Western calligraphy as an art form has not yet been sufficiently understood or appreciated by the general public, in recent years there have been increasing numbers of exhibitions in galleries and museums that focus on lettering.

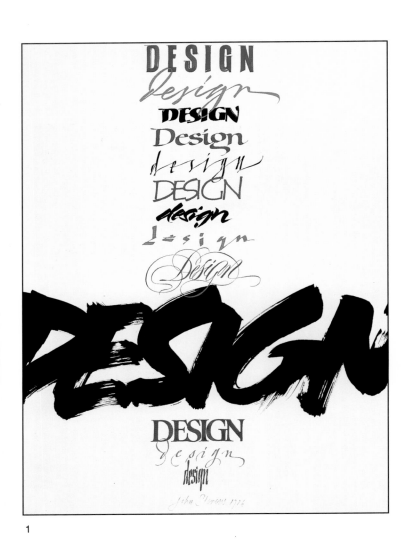

1

2

3

1
John Stevens. *Design*, 1985. 18 x 22. Pens and brushes on paper.
2
John Stevens. *Superlatives*, 1985. 11½ x 21. Pens, brushes, gouache, watercolor, Arches paper.
3
John Stevens. *1987 Headliners Calendar,* 1986. 19 x 24. Various pens, brushes, and quills, casein, gouache, watercolor, on Canson paper. Client: Headliners Identicolor.

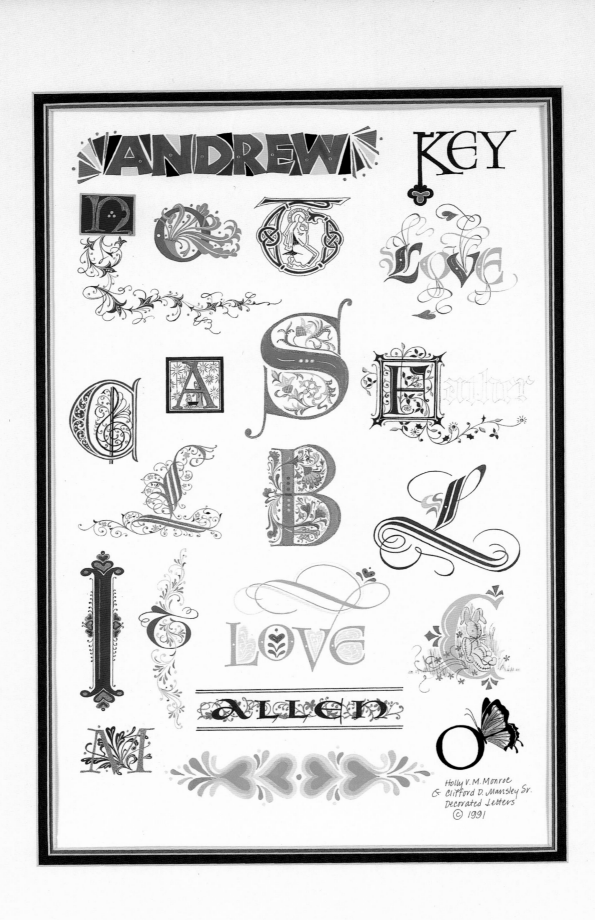

Holly V. M. Monroe
& Clifford D. Mansley Sr.
Decorated Letters
© 1991

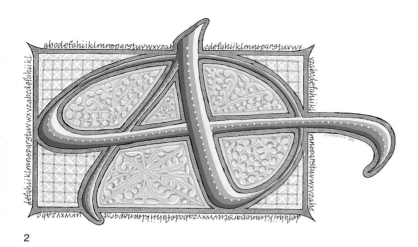

2

3

4

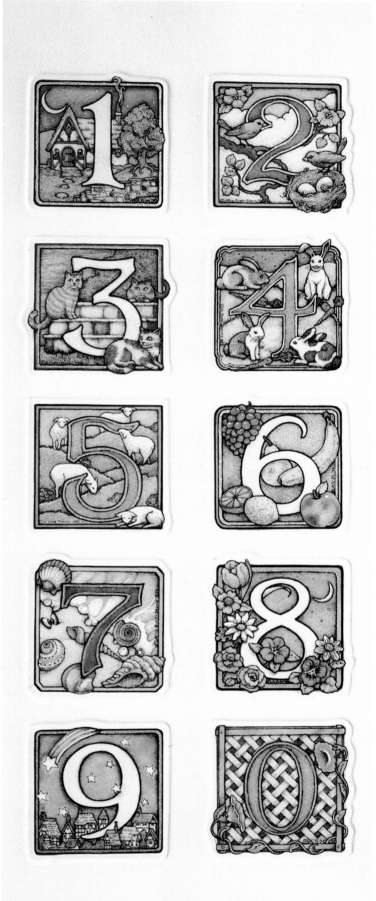

1
Holly V.M. Monroe & Clifford D. Mansley, Sr. *Decorated Letters*, 1991.
Approx. 16 x 20. Brushes, gouache, 24K gold powder.
2
Cheryl O. Adams. *Modern Illuminated "A"*, 1992. 6 x 3½. Rapidograph pen,
ink, gouache, white paint, gold leaf on size, on watercolor paper.
3
Adolf Bernd. *L*, 1991. 5¹⁵⁄₁₆ x 4. Watercolor.
4
Alice Scott-Morris. *Alice's Numbers*, 1992. 7 x 17. Rapidograph on drawing
paper, photo etched into metal plates, printed on printmaking paper, hand
colored with brush and watercolor.

1

Ludo Devaux. *Calligraphy William Morris*, 1992. 60 cm. x 40 cm. Brause
nib, ruling pen, gouache, watercolor, on handmade paper.
2

Marsha Brady. *Untitled*, 1987. 26¼ x 19¾. Brause nibs, dry pigments, on
Roma paper. Author: Rudolf Koch.
3

Michael W. Hughey. *Homage to Rudolf Koch*, 1990. 15 x 18. Original: pen,
ink, on paper. Reproduction: colored inks on Stonehenge paper. Author:
Alfred J. Ludwig. Client: Twin Dolphin Design. Printed by Hewitt Press.
4

John Stevens. *Fractur Improvisation*, 1985. 24 x 18. Pointed brush, colored
Mars markers on white bond paper.

90

ABC DEF GHIJKLM NOP QRSTU VW XYZ

In all the alphabets yet created there lies a wealth, an abundance of possible creative interpretations which we only perceive as we give them more intensive study. The LETTER was formed and to form implies creation.

This is a divine process, even when it takes place within the four walls of a humble workshop. Once, there was someone working at each letter who felt the joy of creation pulsing in his veins. Whoever looks at letters with a receptive eye will therefore sense the miracle which occurs when ever individual signs composing a group become the image of a language, and he will discover a meaningful life in this allegedly dead matter. Alfred J. Ludwig

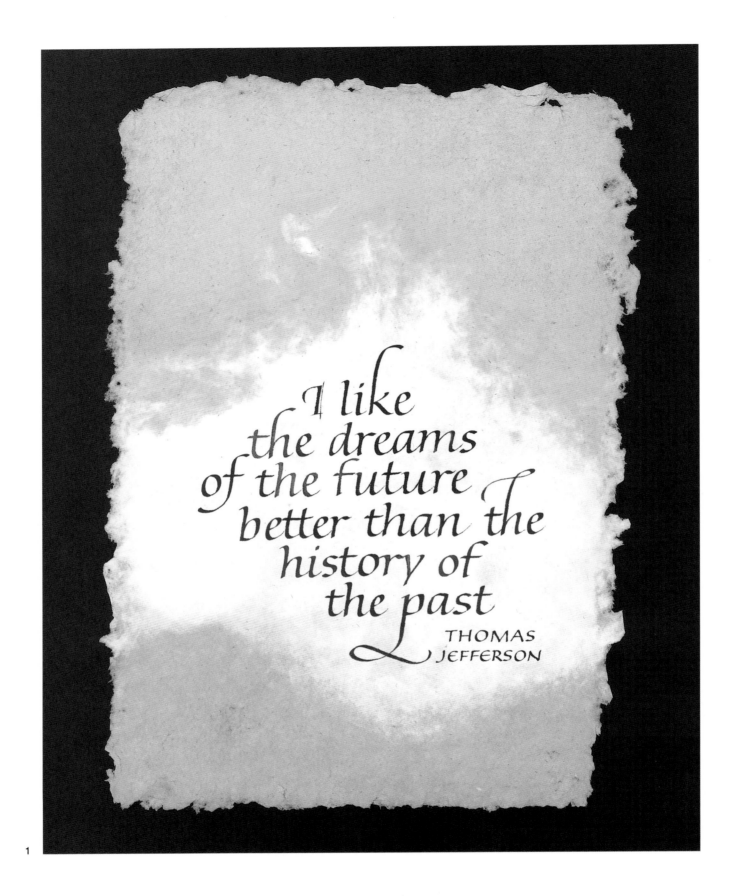

I like
the dreams
of the future
better than the
history of
the past
THOMAS
JEFFERSON

1
Joanne Fink. *Untitled*, 1991. 6 x 9. Rexel nibs, Holbein gouache on
handmade paper. Paper created by Joanne Fink and Janet Hoffberg.
2
Diane M. von Arx. *Art Peace*, 1991. 17½ x 35 framed. Metal nibs, quill,
ruling pen, gouache, India ink, gold leaf, ruling pen on Arches hot press
90 lb. paper. Author: Diane M. von Arx. Photographed by David L. Browne.
3
Terry Englehart. *The Queen Remarked*, 1991. 5⅝ x 10½. Masking fluid
applied with stick, watercolor with brush, on cold press watercolor paper.
Author: Lewis Carroll.

If art is a personal expression or opinion, we must simply take an interest in the art that surrounds us. Interest sparks curiosity, curiosity begs study, study promotes understanding, understanding allows tolerance, and tolerance brings Peace.

The advancement & appreciation of Art must result in Peace.

DIANE M. VON ARX · MINNEAPOLIS

IT'S A POOR SORT OF MEMORY THAT ONLY WORKS BACK WARDS

THE QUEEN REMARKED
LEWIS CARROLL

2

3

1

2

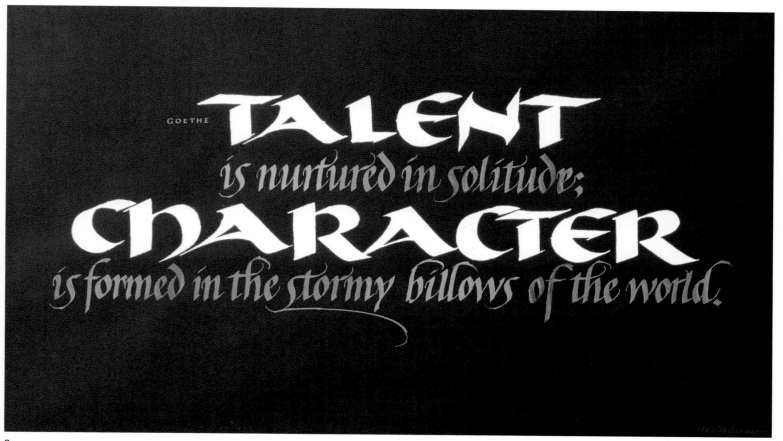

1
Alan Blackman. *First Day Cover Envelope: "Ludwig, The Mad King of Bavaria," Germany*, 1986. Pen and gouache on envelope.
2
Holly V.M. Monroe. *Work is Celebration, Celebration is Work*, 1992. 23 x 14. Mitchell nibs, brush, gouache, silver, Twinrocker paper, Peggy Skycraft hand marbled paper on mat. Client: Libby Sturgés.
3
Michele D. Barnes. *Talent*, 1992. 18 x 10. Coit pen, Rexel nibs, gouache, Pro-White, Canson Mi Tientes paper. Author: Goethe.
4
Ludo Devaux. *Eric Gill Quote*, 1992. 67 cm. x 48 cm. Automatic pens, gouache, on handmade paper. Photographed by Jon De Mylk-Brugge.

1

2

1
Jean Formo. *From the Moment*, 1991. 18 x 52. Brushes, technical pens, colored pencil, fabric pigments, watercolor, on cotton canvas, embellished with ribbons. Author: Bibi Hyati.
2
Annie Cicale, Linda Saucier. *Connecticut Valley Calligraphers Banner*, 1991. 36 x 58. Sign painters' enamel paint on vinyl cloth. Designed by Annie Cicale; enlarged, drawn and painted by Linda Saucier.
3-4
Carol Erickson. *Alphabet Banner,* 1990. 36 x 60. Art tech series 650 brush and Rotring Artists color on primed canvas.

3

4

1

2

1-2
Dick Beasley. *Banner for Center for Excellence, Northern Arizona University*, 1986. 5' x 9'. Acrylic paints on cotton canvas.
3-4
Lisa Engelbrecht. *An Alle Gärtner*, 1990. 36 x 120. Brause nibs, Rotring inks, metallic watercolor, pigment, ruling pen, on unprimed canvas.

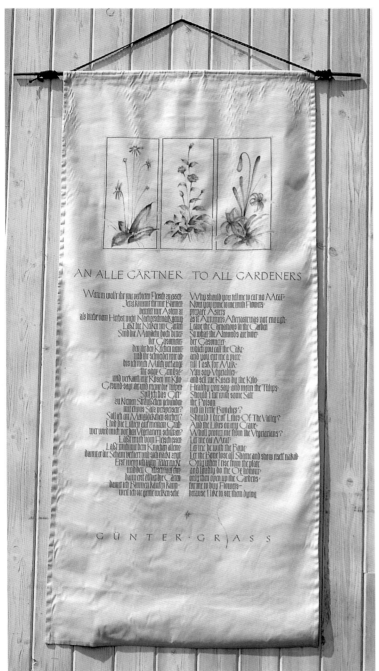

3

4

CATS &
KINGS

With wide unblinking stare,
The cat looked; but she did not see the king.
She only saw a two-legged creature there,
Who, in due time, might have tit-bits to fling.

With swishing tail she lay
And watched for happy accidents, while he,
The essential king, was brooding far away
In his own world with hope and memory.

The gulf might not be wide;
But over it, at least, no cat could spring,
So once again an ancient adage lied,
The cat looked; but she never saw the king.

ALFRED NOYES

1

2

1
Howard Glasser. *Cats & Kings*, 1989. 10 x 14. Steel nibs, gouache, electro-static print with 23K gold leaf, on Vicksburg paper. Author: Alfred Noyes.
2
Howard Glasser. *Ceilidh Uncial*, 1986. 10 x 14. Steel nib, gouache, paper cut. Electrostatic print on Vicksburg paper.
3
Jerry Kelly. *Jan Tschichold*, 1989. 6¾ x 9. Mitchell nibs. Reproduced by photo line engraving, printed letterpress on Moriki paper. Columna and Garamond type. Author: Jan Tschichold. Client: *Q: Quill: Journal of Michigan Association of Calligraphers*. Art Director: Susan Skarsgard.
4
Jerry Kelly. *Bacchus and Cerres*, 1991. 8 x 5¾. Mitchell nibs. Reproduced by photo line engraving, printed letterpress on handmade paper.

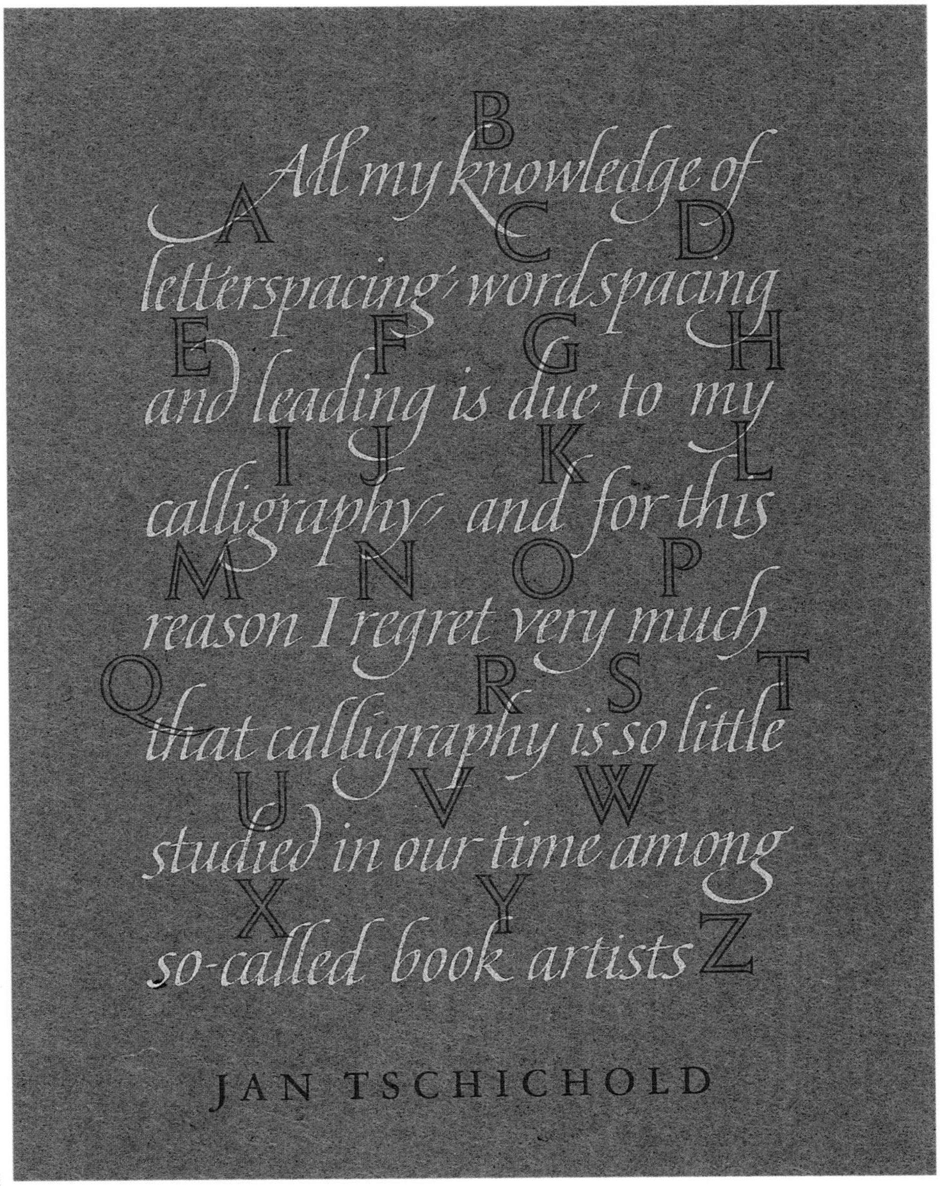

All my knowledge of
letterspacing, wordspacing
and leading is due to my
calligraphy, and for this
reason I regret very much
that calligraphy is so little
studied in our time among
so-called book artists

A B C D E F G H I J K L M N O P Q R S T U V W X Y Z

JAN TSCHICHOLD

3

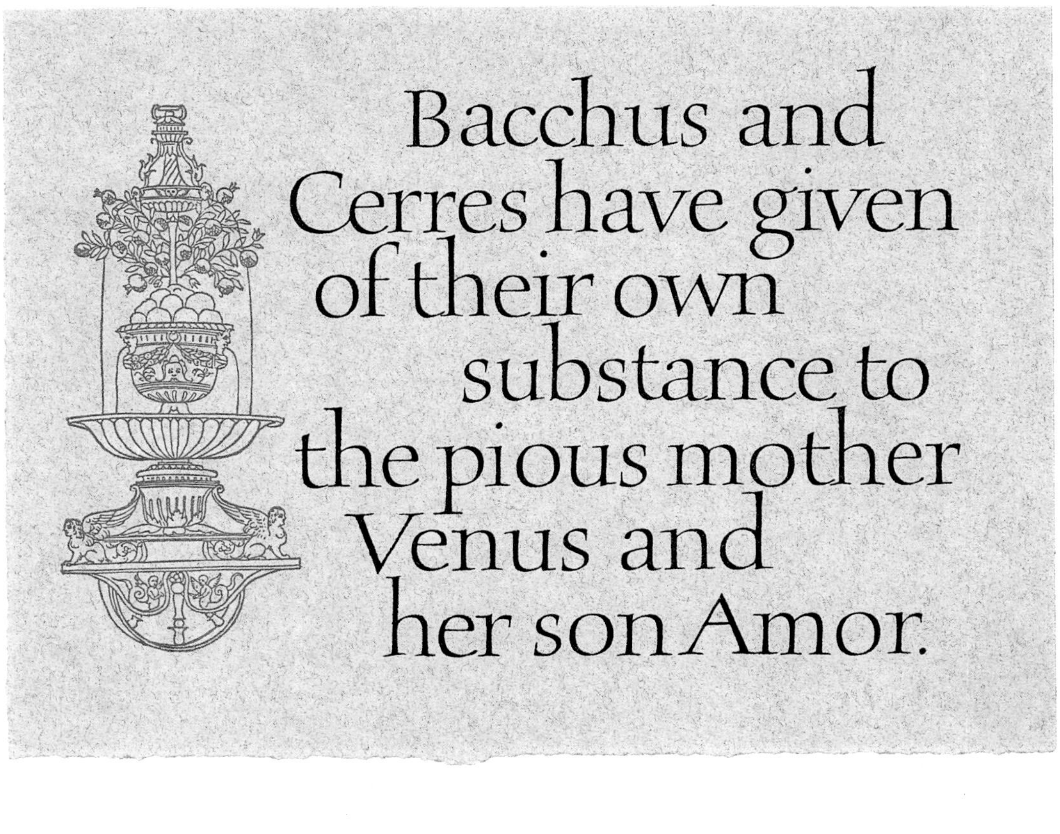

Bacchus and
Cerres have given
of their own
substance to
the pious mother
Venus and
her son Amor.

4

1

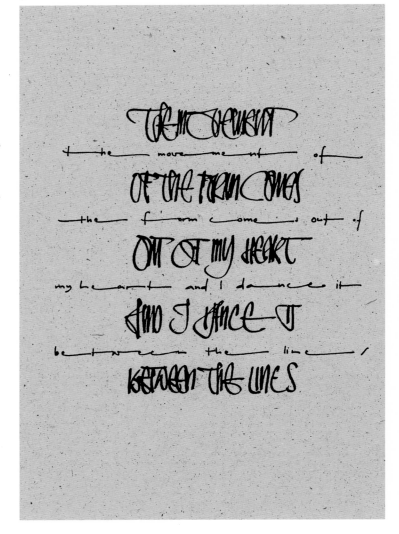

2

3

Letters are symbols which turn matter into spirit.

ALPHONSE DE LAMARTINE

WE USE THE LETTERS OF OUR ALPHABET EVERY DAY WITH THE UTMOST EASE AND UNCONCERN, TAKING THEM ALMOST AS MUCH FOR GRANTED AS THE AIR WE BREATHE. WE DO NOT REALIZE THAT EACH OF THESE LETTERS IS AT OUR SERVICE TODAY ONLY AS THE RESULT OF A LONG AND LABORIOUSLY SLOW PROCESS OF EVOLUTION IN THE AGE-OLD ART OF WRITING. DOUGLAS C. MCMURTRIE

INGRES-FABRIANO

1991 • Marcy Robinson   LETTER ARTS BOOK CLUB KEEPSAKE ©1991 Marcy Robinson. Printed by the Pioneer Press, Terra Alta, W.V. Published by John Neal, Bookseller, 1833 Spring Garden St., Greensboro, NC 27403

4

1
Sherry Bringham. *Quotation by Tagore*, 1991. 7 x 5. Steel nib, colored pencils, PH Martin's Dyes, on Arches paper. Client: Graphic Arts of Marin.
Art Director: Michael Osborne Design, San Francisco, CA.
2
Katharina Pieper. *Here Water-There Water*, 1990. 20 cm. x 50 cm. Redis nib, Sumi ink, Aquarell color, on handmade paper. From *Beginning of a Haiku* by Shiki.
3
Katharina Pieper. *The Movement of the Form*, 1991. 42 cm. x 60 cm. Leather pen and Viet pen, Sumi ink on white scribble paper.
4
Marcy Robinson. *Letters are Symbols*, 1991. Original 10⅜ x 7¼. Speedball C nib, Rexel nibs, black Sumi ink, Hammermill 666 bond paper. Printed on Ingres-Fabriano 9¾ x 7. Authors: Alphonse de Lamartine and Douglas C. McMurtrie. Client: John Neal Bookseller.

nature·first·green·is·gold

her·hardest·hue·to·hold·
her·early·leaf's·a·flower·
but·only·so·an·hour·
Then·leaf·subsides·to·leaf·
So·Eden·sank·to·grief·
So·dawn·goes·down·to·day·
Nothing·gold·can·stay·

robert frost

1

LETS DO IT AFTER
THE HIGH ROMAN
FASHION AND MAKE DEATH
PROUD TO TAKE US.

ANTONY
AND
CLEOPATRA

OH WOMEN COME AWAY
WE HAVE NO FRIEND
BUT RESOLUTION AND THE
BRIEFEST END

2

1
Marijo A. Carney. *Nature's First Green is Gold*, 1990. 24 x 28. Steel pen, gouache, 23K gold leaf on paste and gesso base on birch bark veneer paper. Author: Robert Frost.
2
Jerry Tresser. *Antony and Cleopatra*, 1990. 12 x 18. Quills, ink, variegated gold leaf on Fabriano Roma cream paper.
3
Ludo Devaux. *The Written Letter*, 1992. 33 cm. x 46 cm. Speedball nib, gouache.
4
Elmo van Slingerland. *Untitled*, 1992. 65 cm. x 50 cm. Speedball nib, gouache on Fabriano Italia paper. Author: Paul van Ostayen.

3

4

1

2

EISTEDDFOD
AWARD
MIKE SEEGER

The Eisteddfod Committee of SMU
wishes to express its recognition and
appreciation of your accomplishments
in the study and perpetuation of the
folk arts and ways. Your important
part in the revival of the old-time string
band and your encouragement of
traditional artists have inspired
countless young artists.

A OES HEDDWCH? HEDDWCH!

Chairman, Fred Giftin ~ Archdruid, Howard Glasser September 1989 Southeastern Massachusetts University

3

1
Robert Boyajian. *July Calendar*, 1992. 13 x 18. Brush and flexible pen,
Luma white paint, on Moriki paper.
2
Ilene Winn-Lederer. *Gift Certificate/Pinsker's Judaica Center*, 1989. 9 x 6.
Pen, ink, watercolor, on vellum bristol board. Client: Brad Perelman,
Pinsker's Judaica Center, Pittsburgh, PA.
3
Howard Glasser. *Eisteddfod Award - Mike Seeger*, 1990. 10 x 14. Steel
nibs, gouache, printed on Vicksburg paper. Client: UMD Eisteddfod
Traditional Arts Festival.

1
Dick Beasley. *Award of Distinction, Jenny Holzer*, 1991. Broad-edged nibs, Japanese stick ink, gouache, gold leaf on gum ammoniac size, on handmade Twinrocker paper. Client: National Council of Art Administrators.

2
Dick Beasley. *A Recognition of Merit, Eloise Greenfield*, 1990. 13 x 19. Broad-edged nibs, gouache, gold leaf on gum ammoniac size, on Fabriano Roma paper. Client: The George C. Stone Center for Children's Books, Claremont Graduate School, Claremont, CA.

3
Dick Beasley. *Award of Distinction, Jacinto Quirarte*, 1990. Broad-edged nibs, Rotring inks, gouache, shell gold on Canson and Fabriano Roma papers, with woven strip of vellum. Client: National Council of Art Administrators.

110

2

T O R E I

1
Denis Brown. *"Dublin 1991" Presentations*, 1992. 17 x 24. Lettering with metal nibs; calligraphic abstraction with a three-inch decorator's paint brush. Client: Dublin 1991, European city of culture.
2
John Stevens. *In Heaven and on Earth*, 1990. 11½x 15½. Pointed brush, Sumi ink, on rice paper. Author: Torei.
3
Rick Cusick. *Revelation 3:16 Quote*, 1987. Client: Donald E. Knuth for his book *3:16 Bible Texts Illuminated*, 1991.

Revelation 3:16

Since you are merely lukewarm — neither cold nor hot — I'm going to spit you out of my mouth!

3

1

OF ALL
THE INANIMATE
OBJECTS
OF ALL MEN'S
CREATIONS
BOOKS
ARE THE
NEAREST TO US
FOR THEY
CONTAIN OUR
VERY THOUGHTS,
OUR AMBITIONS,
OUR
INDIGNATIONS,
OUR ILLUSIONS
OUR FIDELITY
TO TRUTH
AND OUR
PERSISTENT
LEANING
TOWARDS ERROR
BUT MOST
OF ALL THEY
RESEMBLE US
IN THEIR
PRECARIOUS
HOLD ON
LIFE

JOSEPH CONRAD

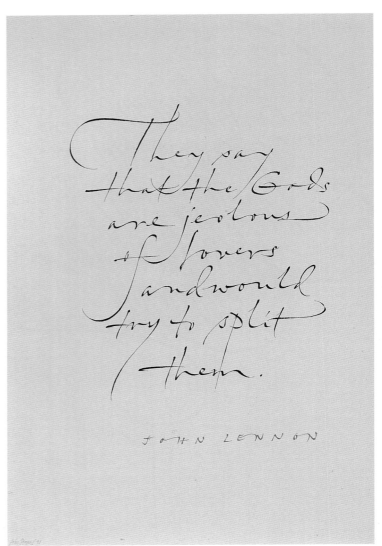

2

1
Sheila Waters. *Books*, 1984. 15 x 22. Speedball C nibs, Chinese stick ink, on handmade paper. Author: Joseph Conrad.
2
John Stevens. *They Say the Gods...*, 1991. 11½ x 15½. Broad-edged pen, Sumi ink and gouache. Author: John Lennon.
3
John Stevens. *Experimental Brush "Calligraphy"*, 1992. 11 x 17. Pointed brush, watercolor on watercolor paper.

3

113

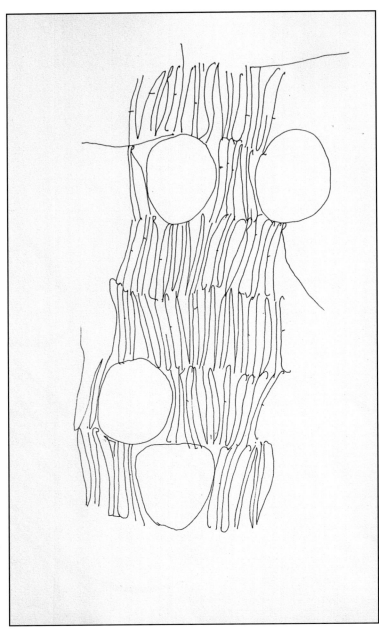

2

1

1
Rick Cusick. *Sacred Song*, 1991. 24½ x 31. Serigraph.
2
Hans-Joachim Burgert. *Habe Ich's Nicht Getroffen*, 1983. Monoline pen and ink, printed by hand letterpress.
Text: Old Testament: From *Ludus Scribendi*, Vol. III.
Translation: "If I have not got it right, teach me better. Look up towards the sky and recognize that the clouds are too high for you."
3
Thomas Ingmire. *Plastic Smiles*, 1992. 6¹¹⁄₁₆ x 10⅜. Ruling pen, ink, paper.
Author: Thomas Ingmire.

OSON OF MAN!
VEILED IN MY
IMMEMORIAL BEING
AND IN THE ANCIENT
ETERNITY OF MY
ESSENCE, I KNEW MY
LOVE FOR THEE;
THEREFORE I CREATED
THEE, HAVE
ENGRAVED ON
THEE MINE IMAGE
AND REVEALED
TO THEE
MY PURPOSE.

Bahá-u-lláh – Hidden Words

1
Keith Eldridge. *Hidden Words*, 1992. 22 x 30. Mitchell nib on Strathmore
paper. Author: Baha'u'llah.

2
Hans-Joachim Burgert. *Wie Tau auf Weissem Marmor,* 1987. Broad-edged
pen and ink; Illustration: lino cut 3-4 colors. Printed by Boston Hand Press.
Text: Flaubert.

3-4
Gail Vick. *Mystery*, 1992. 21 x 29. Colored pencil, watercolor, gold leaf, on
Nideggan paper. Photographed by Keith Bullis.

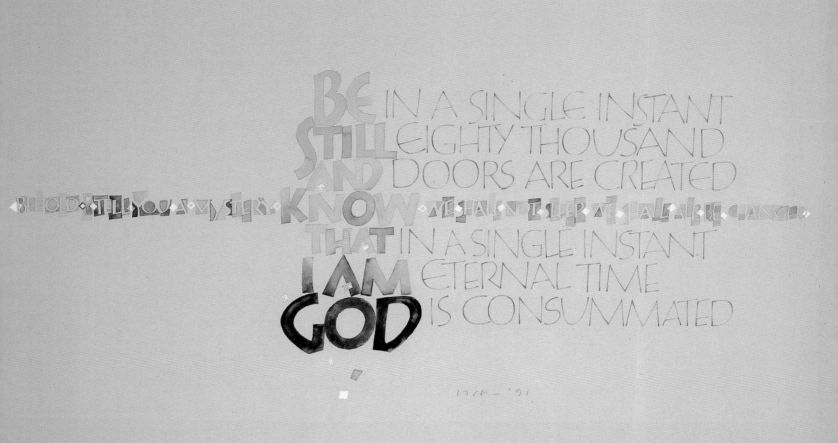

3

4

SOME ASK THE WORLD
AND ARE DIMINISHED
IN THE RECEIVING
OF IT ·

YOU
GAVE ME

ONLY THIS SMALL POOL
THAT THE MORE I DRINK
FROM · THE MORE OVERFLOWS
ME WITH
SOURCELESS
LIGHT ·

GIFT by R.S. thomas

'92

1
Elizabeth McKee. *Gift*, 1992. 10 x 14. Brush, colored pencils, colored inks, gouache, on Indian cotton paper. Author: R. S. Thomas.
2
Gail Vick. *Shadows*, 1990. 16 x 20. Mixed media on canvas. Author: Tagore. Photographed by Keith Bullis.
3
Judy Kastin. *Caring*, 1993. 15 x 11. Pentel Color Brush, Zig Metallic Marker on Arches 140 lb. cold press watercolor paper. Paste paper background: Flashe paints, pastels, wood veneer, popsicle sticks. Author: Judy Kastin. Photographed by Wade Meyer.

1

2

If Music be the
Food of Love, play on.
Give me excess of it; that, surfeiting,
The appetite may sicken, and so die.
That strain again!—it had a dying fall:
O, it came o'er my ear, like the sweet sound
That breathes upon a bank of violets,
Stealing and giving odour! Enough, no more:
'Tis not so sweet now, as it was before.
O Spirit of Love
How quick and fresh art thou,
That, notwithstanding thy capacity
Receiveth as the sea, naught enters there,
Of what validity and pitch soe'er,
But falls into abatement, and low price,
Even in a minute!
So full of Shapes is Fancy
That it alone is high Fantastical.

Twelfth Night — Shakespeare

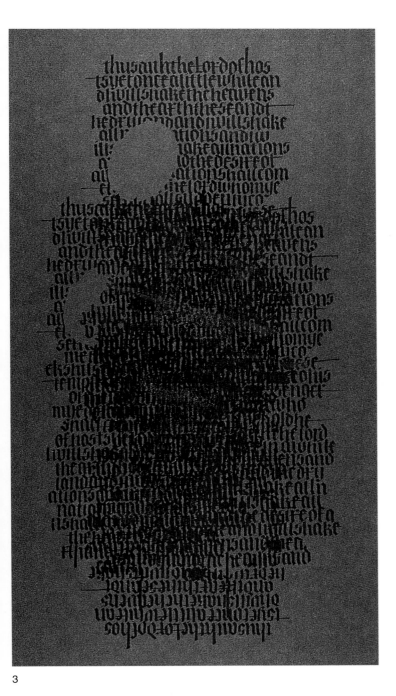

3

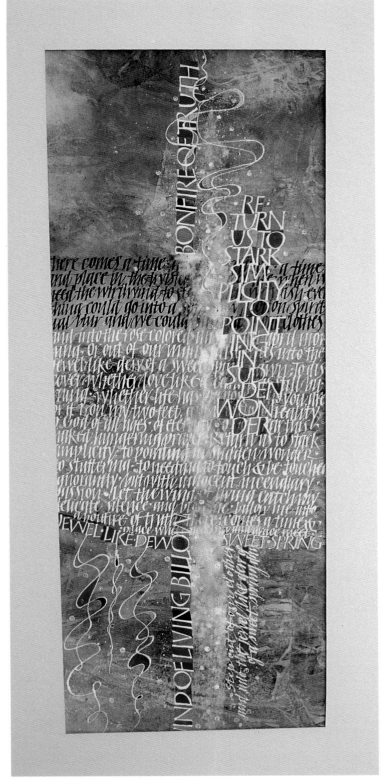

4

1
Marsha Brady. *O Great Spirit*, 1992. 25 x 6½. Brause nibs, gouache, dry pigment, on Larroque handmade paper. Author: Tatanka Yotanka.
2
Eleanor Winters. *If Music be the Food of Love*, 1991. Goode & Co., #84 nib, Higgins Eternal ink. Offset printed, edition of 200.
Text: "Twelfth Night", act 1, scene 1, by William Shakespeare.
3
Peg Carlson. *Shake the Heavens,* 1992. Speedball pens, gouache, copper Omnicrom on pastel paper.
Text: from #5 Recitative for Bass from "The Messiah" by Handel.
4
Rosemary T. Kelly. *Bonfire of Truth*, 1992. 28 x 13. Metal nib, colored pencils, metallic ink, watercolor, gouache, on watercolor paper.
Author: David Sparenberg. Photographed by Michael Kesceg.

THE TEXTURES OF THE LEAVES
ARE MANY AND VARIED,
THEY COMMUNICATE THEMSELVES
THROUGH SIGHT TO IMAGINARY TOUCH,
EXCITING THE FINGERTIPS:
LEAVES COMING INTO
THE TENDEREST FLESH,
SUPERBLY IN THEIR PRIME,
CRISPING TO OLD AGE;
ALL THIS AT THE SAME SEASON
BECAUSE HERE THERE IS NO AUTUMN.
IN THE SHADOWS
THERE ARE DARK BLUE VEILS,
THE INDIGO DREAMS
OF PLANTS FALLEN ASLEEP...
PAUL SCOTT

1

1
Anna Pinto. *Paul Scott Quotation*, 1992. 10 x 8. Various nibs and brushes,
gouache, watercolor inks, on Nideggen paper.
Text: "The Jewel on the Crown" © 1966 by Paul Scott, William Morrow and Company, Inc.
2
Inga S. Dubay. *A Book Is Like a Garden in the Pocket*, 1991. 5⁷⁄₈ x 5⁷⁄₈.
Watercolor, graphite, 23K gold leaf. Arches 140 lb. cold press watercolor
paper. Arab Proverb. Photographed by David Browne.
3-4
Jocelyn Curry. *To Make a Wreath*, 1991. 16 x 20. Mitchell nibs, colored
pencil, graphite, gouache, on handmade linen paper. Author: Jocelyn Curry.

2

3

4

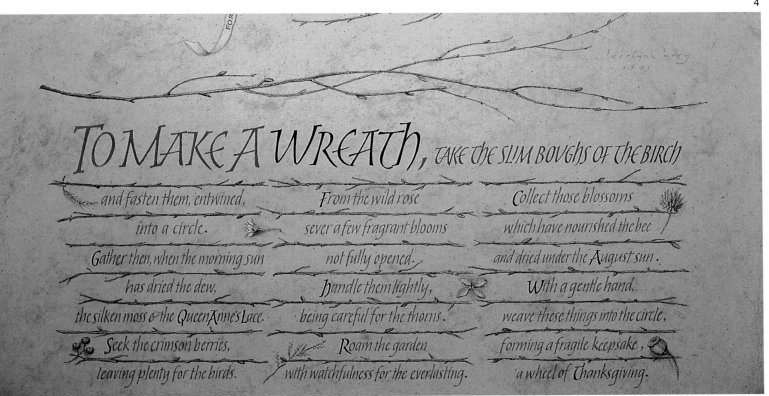

TO MAKE A WREATH, TAKE THE SLIM BOUGHS OF THE BIRCH

and fasten them, entwined,	From the wild rose	Collect those blossoms
into a circle.	sever a few fragrant blooms	which have nourished the bee
Gather then, when the morning sun	not fully opened.	and dried under the August sun.
has dried the dew,	handle them lightly,	With a gentle hand,
the silken moss & the QueenAnne's Lace.	being careful for the thorns.	weave these things into the circle,
Seek the crimson berries,	Roam the garden	forming a fragile keepsake,
leaving plenty for the birds.	with watchfulness for the everlasting.	a wheel of Thanksgiving.

1

Marilyn Reaves. *Join in the General Dance*, 1990. 34⅜ x 22⅛. Prisma Stix, litho crayon and collage on paper.

2-3

Barbara J. Bruene. *Lighthouse*, 1992. 19 x 22. Watercolor, gouache. Author: Elizabeth Bishop.

4

Thomas Ingmire. *Oceans*, 1992. 11 x 6¼. Ruling pen, Sumi ink on paper. Text: "Oceans" by Juan Ramón Jiménez, translated by Robert Bly.

5

Thomas Ingmire. *Wind on an Island,* 1992. 9¾ x 13. Ruling pen, watercolor and gouache, on paper.

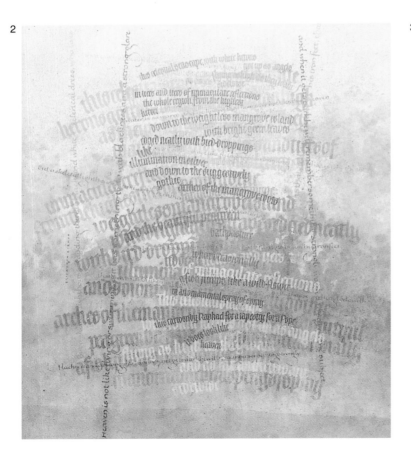

4

5

1-2
Thomas Ingmire. *Metamorphos I and II*, 1992. 20 x 25¾ each. Ruling pen, brushes, watercolor, gouache on paper.
Text: *The Metamorphoses of the Vampire*, by Charles Baudelaire, translated by Geoffrey Wagner.
3
Thomas Ingmire. *Everyone Dances Inside*, 1992. 20 x 25¾. Quills, metal nibs, gouache, watercolor, Pelikan 4001 ink.

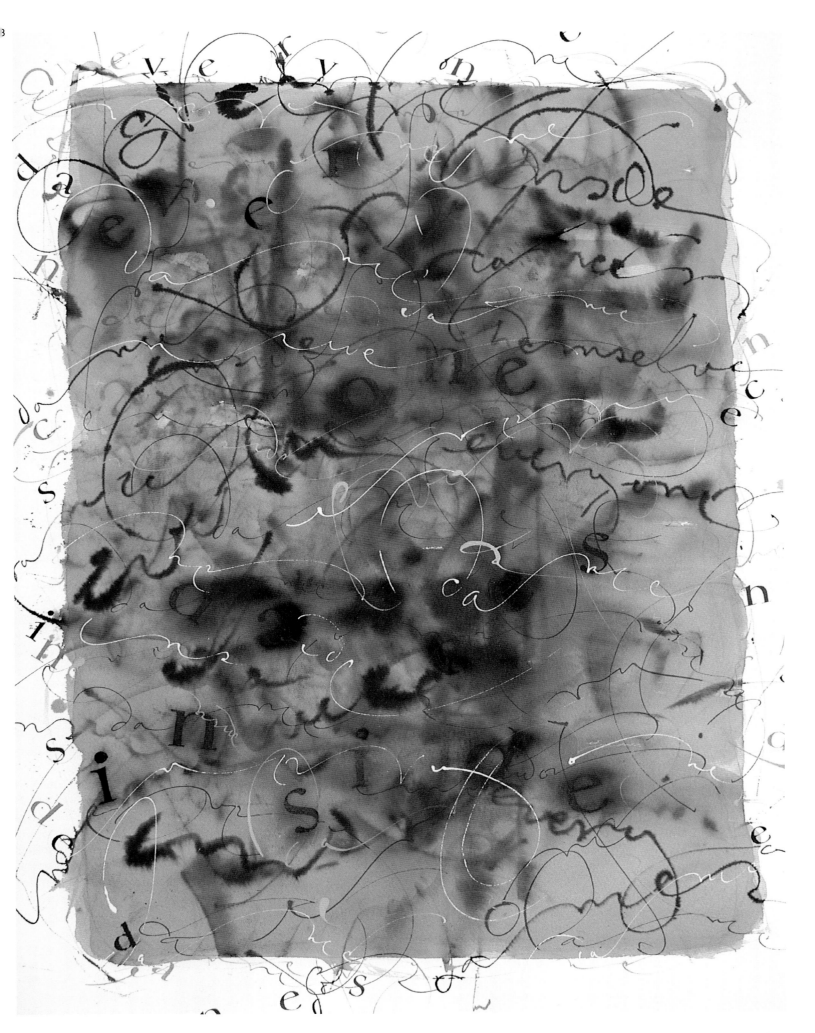

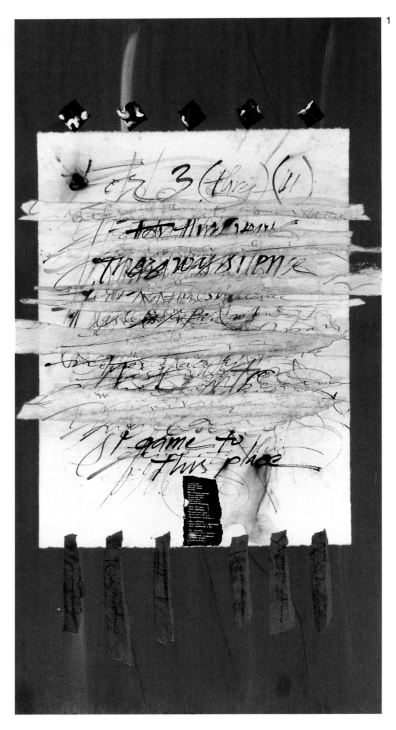

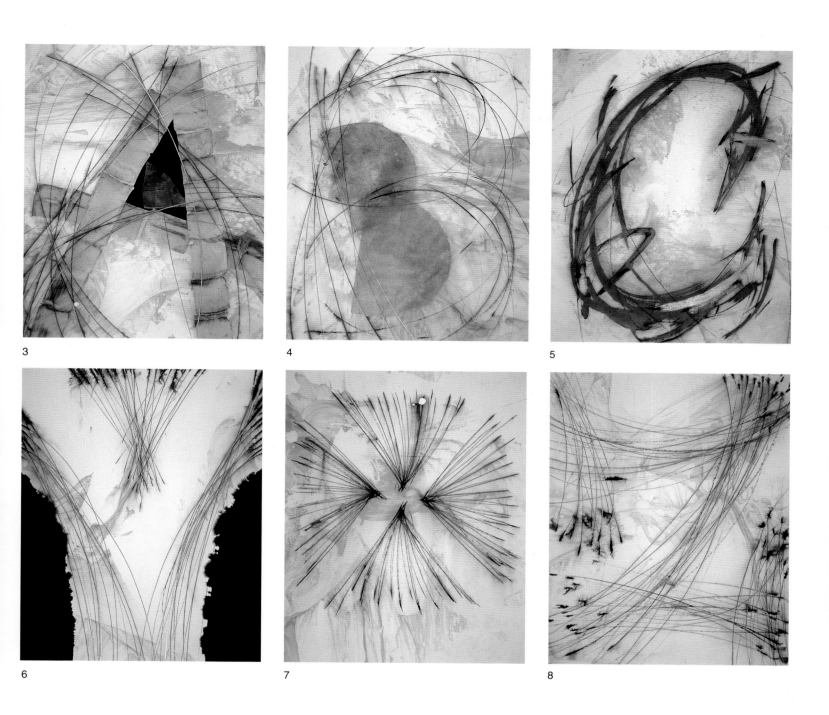

3

4

5

6

7

8

1-2
Steven Skaggs. *Speak*, 1992. 24 x 48. Ink, gouache, and paper, on plywood. Author: Steven Skaggs. Dedicated to Dick Beasley.
Text: For three years there was silence, not that silence is a void— When it became necessary, became imperative to ask why these or any words were required, I came to this place. With the rain came reflection. The need wasn't felt. No one was waiting. The directive never came. Any utterance would have been dishonest, any statement a lie. An alphabet was taken from the shelf, returned unopened placed under lock and key.
3-8
Susan Skarsgard. *Alphabetic Fiction*, 1992. 20 x 25½ (each). Pens, brushes, Sumi ink, gouache, gesso, gold leaf on Arches Text Wove paper.

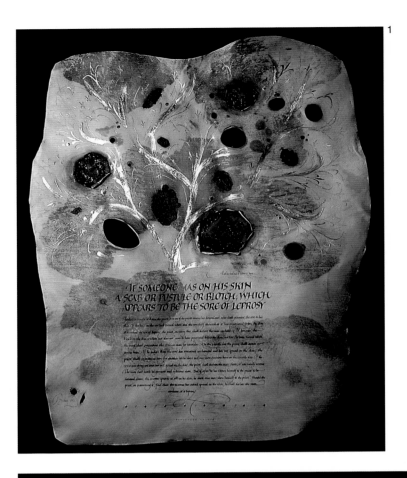

1

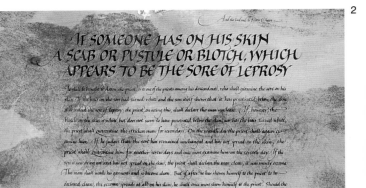

2

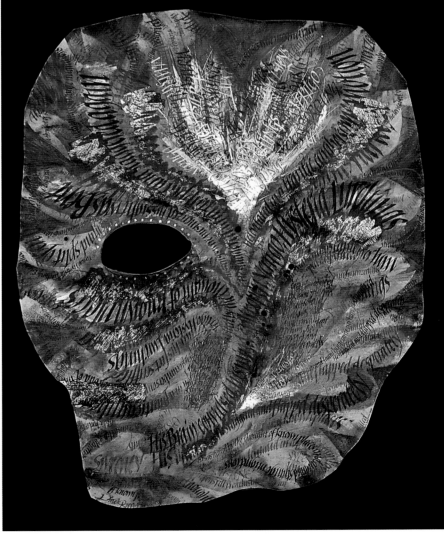

3

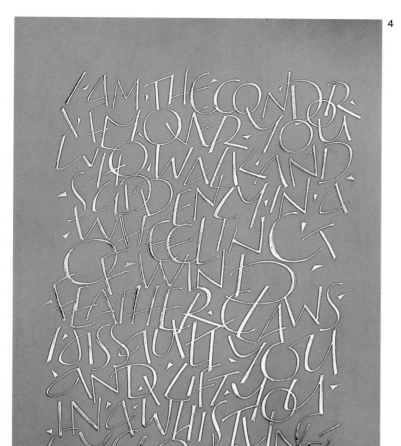

1-2
Denis Brown. *Skin with Elegantly Written Text on Leprosy*, 1992. 32½ x 26½.
Ink, bronze powder, shell gold, gold and copper leaf gilded onto gesso, gum
and impasto medium, gouache, ash, acrylic, gloss, varnish on a calfskin vellum.
3
Denis Brown. *Head of Sweeney*, 1990. 27½ x 22. Ink, gouache, shell gold,
gold leaf on gum and gesso bases on the skin of a stillborn calf.
4
Thomas Ingmire. *The Condor* (Gold), 1990. 12 x 18. Quills, gold powder
and gold leaf on gesso base, on vellum. Author: Pablo Neruda, translated
by Donald D. Walsh.
5
Thomas Ingmire. *The Condor I*, 1989. 12 x 18. Goose quills, Chinese stick
ink, gold leaf on gesso base, on paper. Author: Pablo Neruda, translated by
Donald D. Walsh.

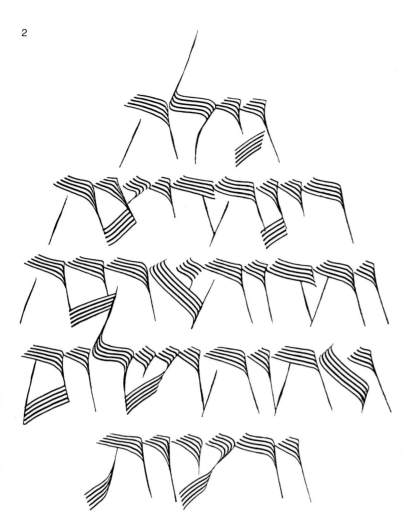

1
Ted S. Kadin. *Oval Ketubah*, 1990. 17 x 24. Mitchell nibs, Higgins Eternal ink, gouache, Winsor & Newton watercolor, technical pen and ink, colored pencil, and airbrush. Client: Helen Sher.

2
Lynn Broide. *Gila Rina*, 1991. 5¼ x 7¾. Coit pen. From blessings of the Jewish marriage ceremony. Client: Dina and Ron Schuster.
Translation: "joy, jubilation, delight, cheer, love, brotherhood, peace and friendship."

3
Leonid Pronenko. *Russian Fairytale*. Pen and Flowmaster ink.

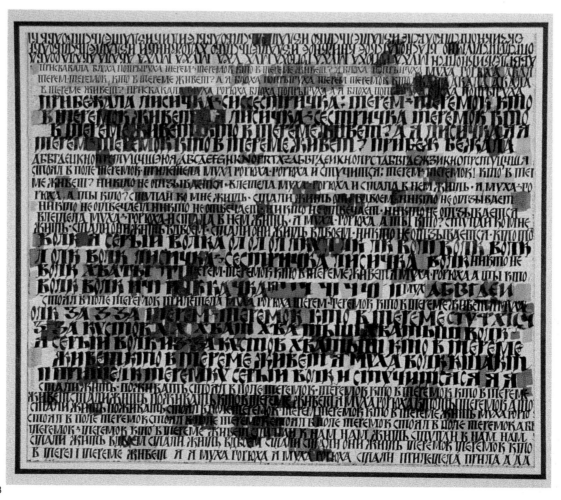

3

1
Elana Weinberg. *Shehechianu*, 1992. 4 x 6. Mitchell nibs, Higgins Eternal ink, #11 X-acto blades, laser cut paper, Martin's inks, on hand-torn rice paper, Gilbert paper.
2
Elana Weinberg. *Priestly Blessing*, 1991. 6 x 10. Mitchell nibs, Higgins Eternal ink, #11 X-acto blades, Martin's inks, on hand-torn rice paper.
Translation: "May the Lord bless you and keep you; May the Lord let his countenance shine upon you and be gracious unto you; May the Lord let his countenance shine upon you and grant you peace."
3
Avraham Cohen. *A Celebration of Letters*, 1991. 11 x 15. Automatic pen, Mitchell nib, brush, watercolor and gouache, gold and silver leaf on a gesso base, on Twinrocker handmade paper.
Text: Hebrew alphabet (two times).

Avraham Cohen ז״ל ©1991

1

1
Mordechai Rosenstein. *Teach*, 1992. 24 x 30. Brush and gouache on Arches 300 lb. mould made paper. Serigraph, oil based inks.
Text: Deuteronomy 6:7.
Translation: "Teach them diligently unto thy children."
2
Mordechai Rosenstein. *Jonah*, 1992. 11 x 14. Oil pastel, gouache, gold tea-chest foil on Arches 300 lb. cold press watercolor paper.
3
Abdul Lateef Madaki. *The Islamic Art of Calligraphy*.
4
Abdul Lateef Madaki. *For Peace*, 1991. 18 x 25. Reed pens, black India ink and white indian poster color on black and white papers. Verse from Holy Quran. Client: T.T.Q., Inc.
Translation: "Prepare any (military) strength you can muster against them, and any cavalry posts with which you can overawe God's enemy and your own enemy as well, plus others besides them whom you do not know. God however knows them!" (Translation by Dr. Thomas B. Irving).

2

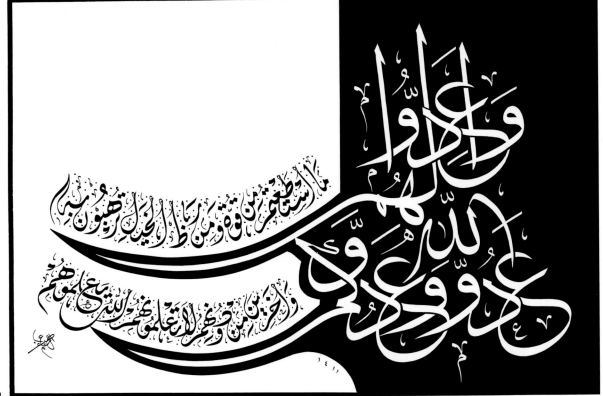

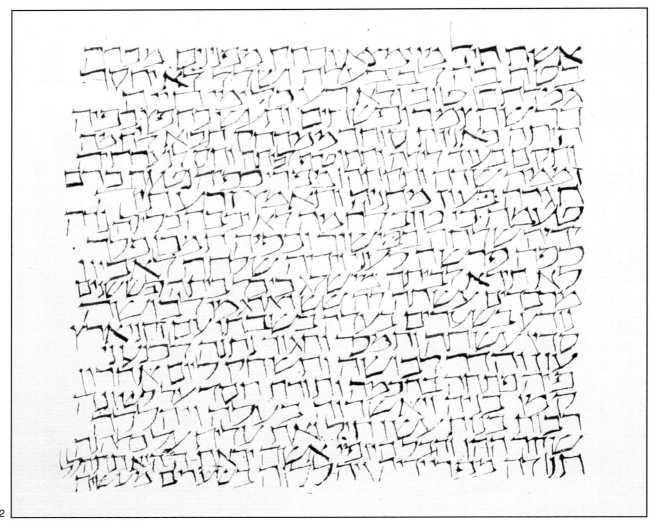

1
Lynn Broide. *Eliyahu*, 1992. 6¼ x 4½. Coit pen and ink.

2
Lynn Broide. Aishet Hayil (A Woman of Valor), 1992, in progress. 12 x 10¼.
Speedball nibs, on Roma Fabriano paper.
Text: King Solomon, Proverbs 31.

3
Siegmund Forst. *Prayer at the River*. 9 x 7. Pen and ink.

4
Lynn Broide. *Ad D'Lo Yada ('Til One Knows Not)*, 1987. 6 x 10 ½.
Coit pens, ink.
Text: Talmud, Masechet Megila - Chapter 1.

1

 אני לדודי ודודי לי · I AM · MY · BELOVED'S · AND · MY · BELOVED · IS · MINE

This Ketubah witnesses before God and all those present that on the first day of the week, the _____ day of the month _____, in the year 5____, which corresponds to the _____ day of the month _____, in the year ____, the holy covenant of marriage was entered into in _____ between the groom _____ and the bride _____. And each said to the other: "I promise to share with you in times of joy as in times of trouble· To talk and to listen, to honor and to appreciate you, to provide for and support you in trust and in love· I take you to be mine according to the laws of Moses and Israel· I promise to share my hopes and thoughts and dreams with you· I will work with you to build our lives together· May we grow... our lives forever intertwined, our love bringing us closer· Let us create a home for us and for our children based on love, on Torah and on the traditions of our Jewish heritage·May it be a home filled with peace, with happiness and with love·"

2

140

3

1
Joanne Fink. *Dodi Li Ketubah*, 1991. 17 x 17. Powell pens, Rexel nibs,
Winsor & Newton series 7 brushes, Holbein gouache, Chinese stick ink on
Strathmore bristol board. Printed 4-color process on 65 lb. Astrolite smooth
cover. Printed by Jeff Langendorf, Manhattan Color.
2
Sivia Katz. *Chupah Ketubah*, 1991. 18 x 18. Sable brushes, Utrecht and
Winsor & Newton watercolors on 140 lb. Arches watercolor paper. Printed in
4-color process on Strathmore paper.
3
Luba Bar-Menachem. *Aishet Hayil (A Woman of Valor)*, 1989. 19 diameter.
Canson paper cut with a scalpel, gouache, gold paint. Print of original papercut.
Text: King Solomon, Proverbs 31: 10-22.

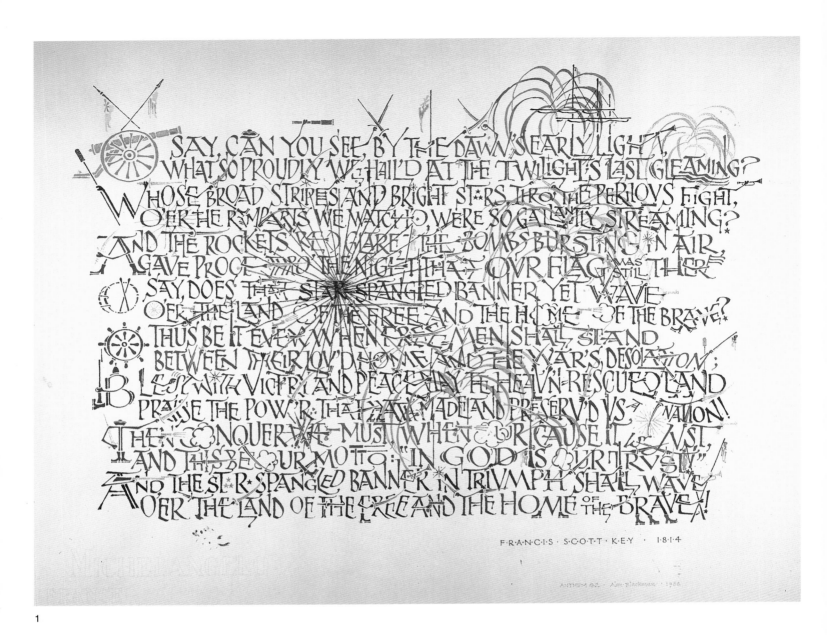

FRANCIS · SCOTT · KEY · 1814

1

1
Alan Blackman. *Star Spangled Banner*, 1988. 26 x 20. Quill, brush, stick ink, gold leaf, gold and silver gouache on Michelangelo paper. Author: Francis Scott Key.
2-3
Jill Overley. *M* and *Z*, 1992. 8½ x 11. Computer generated photo-silkscreens. Letters written or drawn on paper then digitized with a LightningScan 400 hand-held scanner and modified in the scanner software using Deneba's "Canvas" graphics program on an Apple MacIntosh IIcx. Other letters written freehand on a Wacom SD 510 pressure sensitive graphics tablet, using the Wacom application "Pressure Paint", then imported into "Canvas". The images were printed on a Hewlett Packard PaintWriter.

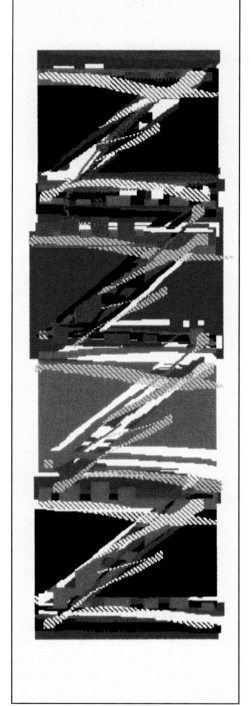

3

2

1

2

3

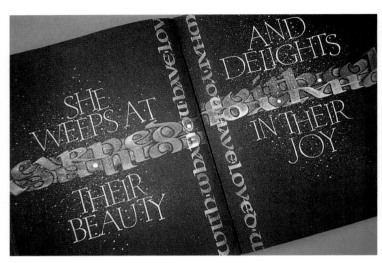

4

1–4

Jean Formo. *Another Language*, 1992. Closed, 9 x 12½. 15 pages.
Handmade book bound in traditional longstitch. Flat brushes, colored pencil,
gouache, acrylic, patent gold on fused black canvas, decorative threads,
buttons, beads.
Text: Poetry by Jean Formo and George Seferis.
5

Dick Beasley. *Untitled*. Broad-edged nibs, graphite, colored pencils, various
inks, gouache, Rotring inks, sink art, and collage.
6

Dick Beasley. *Calligraphic Square,* 1990. 24¼ x 24¼. Brushes, oil and
gold leaf on masonite.

5

6

1
Dick Beasley. *Portrait*, 1991. Computer generated image from scanned, digitized photographs and broad-edged pen.
2
Dick Beasley. *Compubets*, 1991. 28¼ x 22¼. Computer generated image from digitized metal pen and brush work on paper.
3
Dick Beasley. *Untitled*, 1990. Broad-edged nibs, Rotring inks, gold leaf on gum ammoniac size, and sink art on Rives Arches cold press watercolor paper.
4
Dick Beasley. *Untitled*, 1991. Computer generated image from digitized metal pen and brush work on paper.

2

3

4

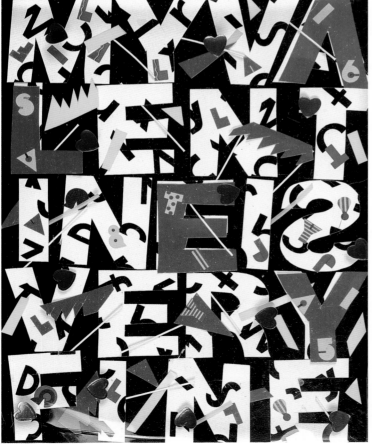

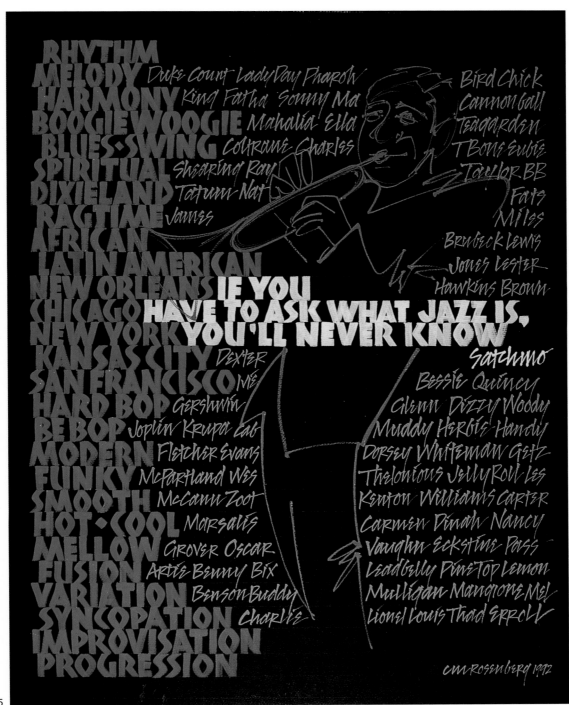

5

1
Carl Rohrs. *Light Mischief, No. 2* (Krazy Kat), 1989. 23 x 29. Pointed brush, flat brushes (for illustration only), colored pencils, gouache on Roma paper. Author: Jay Cantor. Photographed by Bill Reynolds, Dancing Man Imagery. Collection of Deb Slade. A variation of this piece appeared in *Calligraphy Review 1989 Annual*.

2
Marilyn Reaves. *Love*, from a series *Do Ten Things and Lump the Rest*, 1990. 19¾ x 13⅛. Acrylics, gouache, graphite, colored pencil and collage on silk-screened flat, on Arches cover paper.
Main Text reads: Lesson 1. amour (epithemia); 2. eros, 3. philia; 4. agape; 5. caritas.

3
Anna Wolf. *My Valentine*, 1992. 8 x 10. Collage of various cutout letters and shapes, on black velvet background, contained in plastic box.
Text: "My Valentine" by Gertrude Stein.

4
Reggie Ezell. *Sapphire Tide*, 1989. 12 x 18 x 5. Watercolor paper stained with inks, cut black paper, lighted in deep lacquered frame/box. Author: Ezra Pound.

5
Carol Rosenberg. *What's Jazz?* 1992. 20 x 25. Pointed and flat brushes, gouache. Client: The Western Reserve Calligrapher's Communiqué Newsletter.

2

3

1
Lawrence Brady. *Experimental I*, 1991. 8½ x 11. Ruling pen, bamboo pen, Brause nibs, prisma color pencils, stick ink, watercolor, xerography, color tag on bond paper.

2-3
Glen Epstein. *Einsatzgruppen 1 and 2*, 1992. 20½ x 28, 20½ x 27. Ruling pen, pencil, pointed brush, watercolor, gouache, masking fluid, on hand-made paper by Tim Barrett, University of Iowa Center for the Book.

Translation: Einsatzgruppen #1: Special action squads (this was the euphemism for Nazi killing squads prior to mass gas extermination.) Names of places where the above took place. The girl is based on an Egon Schiele painting. Einsatzgruppen #2: Special action squads. Names of towns and villages.

1

2

1
Rory P. Kotin. *Images*, 1991. Open, 49⅝ x 8½. Canson torn paper, Japanese lace paper, tracing vellum, gouache. Author: John Russell.
2
Alan Blackman. *Jabberwocky*, 1987. 26 x 20. Quill, day-glo poster paints on Michelangelo paper. Author: Lewis Carroll.
3-4
Leana Fay. *Hebrews eleven*, 1992. 26 x 28. Acrylic and collage on canvas, palladium on gum ammoniac.

ues in which not everything is explained im

1
Marcy Robinson. *Owen Johnsen*, Distinguished Service Award, 1992.
12 x 16. Speedball C nib, Rexel nibs, Winsor & Newton gouache and gold leaf. Client: The New York Zoological Society. Art Director: Ron Davis.
2
Marcy Robinson. *I Feel an Affinity*, 1992. 12 x 16. Rexel nib and Winsor & Newton gouache. Author: Brooke Astor. Client: The New York Zoological Society. Art Director: Ron Davis. Photo: New York Zoological Society.
3-6
Michael Clark. *Soften My Heart O Lord*, 1991. Booklet. Closed, 5 x 7.
(3) Pigma pen on bond paper (4) Ruling pen, Dr. Martin's dyes, bond paper, Galliard type (5) Ruling pen, black ink, bond paper, Galliard type (6) Mitchell nibs, black ink on bond paper.

1

2

3

WO
DER
GEIST
DES
HERRN
IST,
DA IST
FREIHEIT

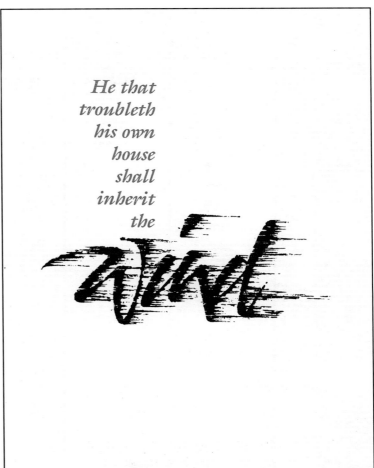

4

He that
troubleth
his own
house
shall
inherit
the
wind

I WILL PUT MY LAWS ON THEIR HEARTS,

and in
their minds
I will write
them

5

God is constantly
seeking out man·
man is forever
in search of God·
IN THE EYES OF
CHILDREN
the path is often
illuminated·

6

1
Stan A. Jones. *Parts of an Heraldic Achievement*, 1991. 10 x 16. Rexel Mitchell nibs #3 and #5 on Carlyle Japan paper. Winsor & Newton designers gouache for illustrations and lettering. For gilding, 23K transfer gold has been applied to a base of acrylic medium gloss.
2
Jerry Tresser. *Wild Thing*, 1990. 12 x 14. Quills, brush, gold, gold size, on handmade Duchine paper.
3
Diane Amarotico. *Alles ist*, 1989. 10 x 10. Technical pen, crayon, on Fabriano paper. Author: Paul Celan.
4
Marilyn Reaves. *Alphabet Journal*, 1992. 9 x 9½. Colored pencil, ink, watercolor, gouache, graphite and collage on Frankfurt cream paper.

3

4

1

2

3

1- 3
Judy Mueller. *Stars and Stripes for Tommy Feng*, 1990. 8 x 18 x 2. Letters cut from multiple layers of foam board faced by mat board, stars are gouache. Letters are suspended from and tethered by brass swivels. Authors: Yi Feng and Qibing Hu. Collection of Qibing Hu and Yi Feng.

4
Mary White. *Untitled*, 1992. 25 cm. x 25 cm. x 8 cm. Boxed crater form with colored porcelain inside and mirror. Letters painted in black oxide.

5
Mary White. *Untitled*, 1992. 25 cm. x 25 cm. x 8 cm. Boxed crater form with mirror. Painted letters in black oxide, fired to 1250 degrees but unglazed. Slab method.

6- 7
Mary White. *Untitled*, 1992. 10 cm. x 10 cm. x 10 cm. Cube with relief letterforms. Unglazed.

4

5

6

7

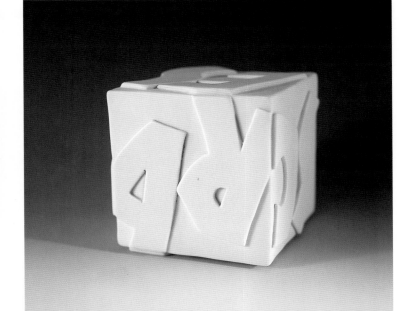

1-3
Linda P. Levine. *Chief Seattle*, 1990. Closed, 7 x 11. Open, 41 x 4½. Metal pens, stick ink, gouache, watercolor and rubber stamps made by the artist. Photographed by Steve Halperson.
Text: "Pushing Up the Sky" from *American Indian Myths & Legends*, Erdoes & Ortiz, eds.

4-6
Jenny Hunter Groat. *A Vision:* multiple-scroll book sculpture, 1992. Closed, 12 x 9 x 3. Open, 16 x 9 x 25. Pointed brush, Chinese stick ink, Chinese and Japanese papers, gold tea chest paper, redwood seed cones, redwood bark, other flora from California redwood forest. Mat board, linen threads, hand carved redwood latches. © 1992 Jenny Hunter Groat. Permanent Collection, The National Museum of Women in the Arts, Washington, D.C.
Text: Wendell Berry: six short poems from *A Part;* title poem "A Vision" (large, seventh scroll) from *Collected Poems:* "Worksong", courtesy of North Point Press.

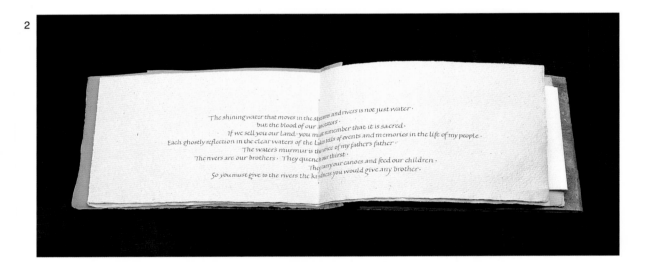

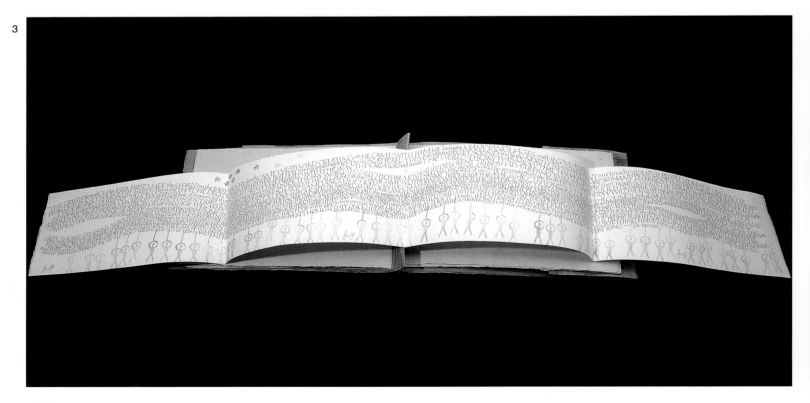

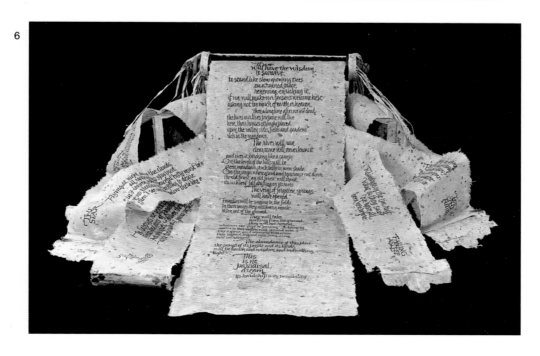

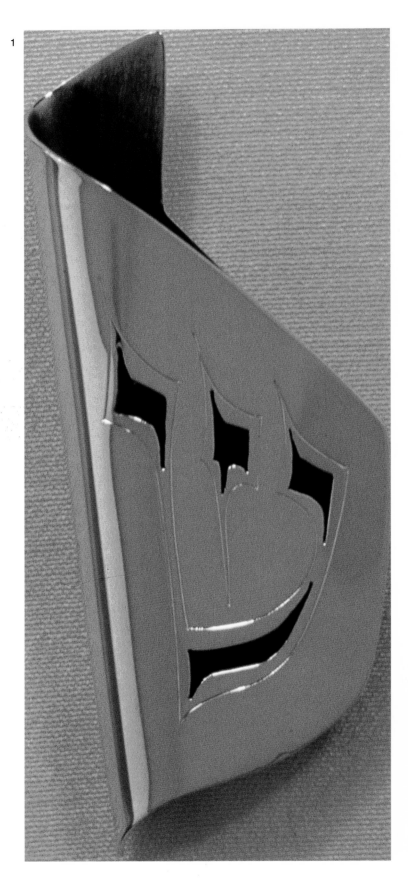

1

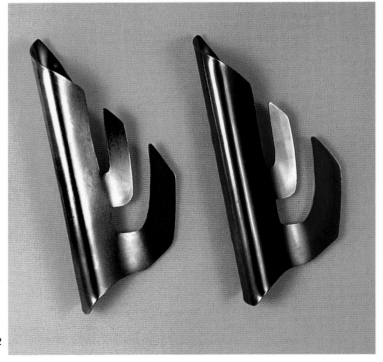

1

Chava Wolpert Richard. *Mezuzah Case*, 1990. 1¼ wide x 3⅜ high x 9⁄16 deep. Fabricated silver. Hebrew letter is pierced (cut with jeweler's saw) and partially engraved.

Translation: The Hebrew letter *shin* stands for the word *Shaddai*, "the Almighty."

2

Chava Wolpert Richard. *Shin Mezuzah Case*, 1992. 1½ high x 3¾ wide x ½ deep. Anodized aluminum, fabricated.

Translation: The Hebrew letter *shin* stands for the word *Shaddai*, "the Almighty."

3

Chava Wolpert Richard. *High Holidays Prayer Book Cover*, 1980. Open, 11¾ x 8¼. 24K gold cloisonne enamel on fine silver, bound in leather. Collection of Mr. and Mrs. Joseph Lepelstat.

Text: Psalms 113: 9.

Translation: "Who maketh the barren woman to dwell in her house as a joyful mother of children. Hallelujah."

2

3

THAT IS THE PRIMAL ACT OF CREATION: TO SUMMON FORTH SPIRIT FROM OUT OF LIFELESS MATTER

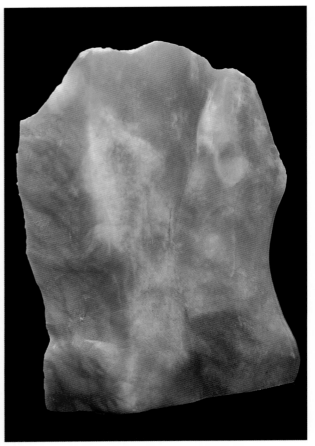

2

3

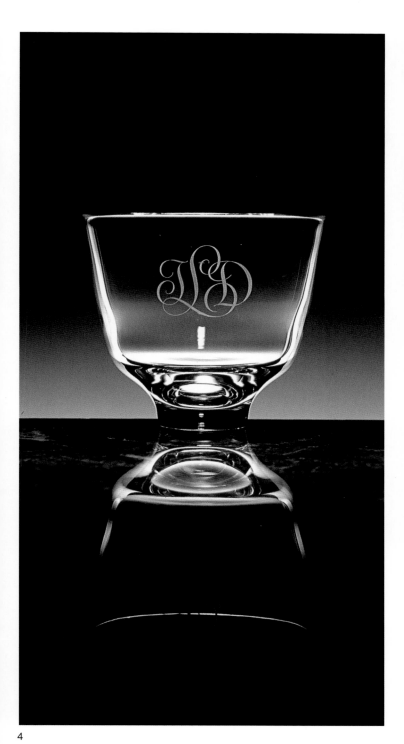

4

5

1-2
Reggie Ezell. *Spirit from Matter*, 1990. 10 x 15 x 5. Chisels, hammer,
X-acto knife blades, power tools, Utah alabaster. Author: Reggie Ezell.
3
Mark Van Stone. *The Ptolemy Palette*, 1987. 10 x 13. Steel chisels, carved
slate.
4
Patricia Weisberg. *Monogrammed Medium Cup-Shaped Bowl.* 7⅛ diameter
x 6¾ high. Original: Drawn with pencil, letters filled in with pointed brush
and ink on bond paper. Lettering sandblasted onto glass. Client:
Steuben Glass. Photographed by Roger Moore.
5
Judy Mueller. *Advice*, 1990. 7¾ x 5¾ x 3¼. Commercial building brick
masked and etched, additional etching with hand-held diamond point tools.
Text: *(obverse)* People who live in glass houses *(reverse)* should learn to make Windex.

SELECT LETTERING ARTS

Growing interest in calligraphy led to the 1982 publication of *Calligraphy Review* (originally titled *Calligraphy Idea Exchange*), a quarterly journal dedicated to the calligraphic arts. Each issue features historical and contemporary works from all parts of the world.

Under the direction of publisher Karyn Gilman, the content appeals to amateur and professional calligraphers as well as to graphic artists. Experimental and traditional pieces in a variety of media reveal the diversity of lettering arts past and present. Western and non-Western works are featured alongside profiles of leading calligraphers, articles on theory and practice, detailed book reviews and general information.

One of the magazine's most significant contributions has been the creation of its own juried competition, the "Annual Review." Each year, top professionals in the fields of lettering and the related arts make selections from hundreds of entries received. The *Annual Review* issue is extremely popular as it chronicles current trends in lettering design.

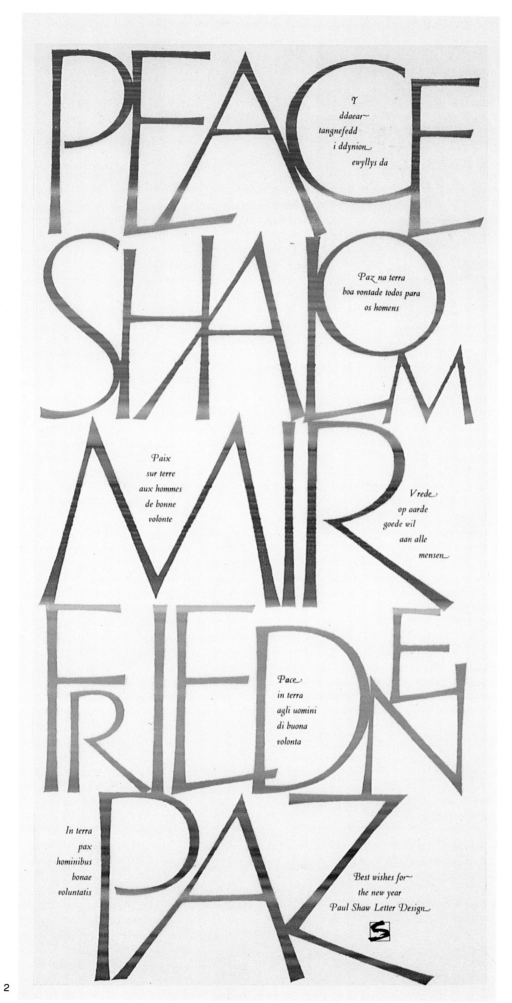

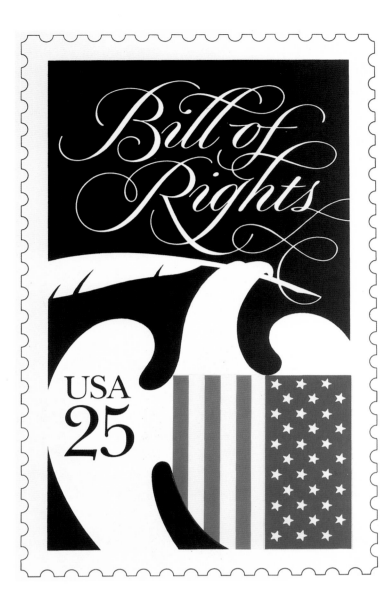

1

3

1
Julian Waters. *Bill of Rights Stamp*, 1988. Printed stamp 1 x 1½. Pointed pen, pointed brush, Chinese stick ink on smooth bond paper. Client: U. S. Postal Service. Art Director: Derry Noyes. Designer: Lou Nolan. *1990 Annual.*

2
Georgia Deaver. *Le Champ Champagne Label*, 1983. Pointed brush on watercolor paper. Client: © Le Champ Cellars. Art Director: Cal Anderson. *Vol. 2, #3, 1985.*

3
Lawrence R. Brady. *Lavosh Hawaii*, 1989. Original: 11½ x 9. Brause nibs, reed pens, brushes, gouache, Dr. PH Martin's Radiant Concentrated Watercolors, on Arches 140 lb. cold press watercolor paper. Client: Adrienne's Gourmet Foods. *1989 Annual.*

4
Sherry Bringham. *Capture the Holiday Spirit*, 1990. 11 x 8½. Chinese pointed brush, stick inks, Arches paper. Client: © Charles King Winery of the Seagrams Classics Wine Co. Art Director: Sandy Cooper, The Ram Group. *1990 Annual.*

5
Alan Blackman. *Happy Birthday #1*, 1983. Open, 15 x 7. Brush, pencil, gouache. Client: Pegasus Press, Berkeley, CA. *1988 Annual.*

6
Alan Blackman. *Happy Birthday #2*, 1985. Open, 15 x 7. Brush, pencil, gouache. Client: Pegasus Press, Berkeley, CA. *1988 Annual.*

4

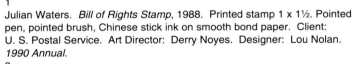

5

6

If you can
survive
a Chicago
winter,
you can
make it
through
life

1

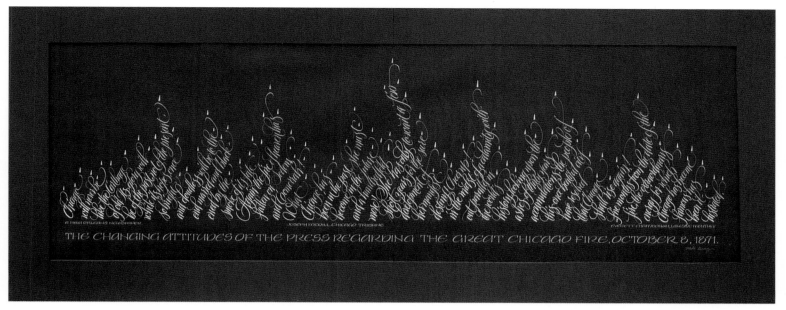

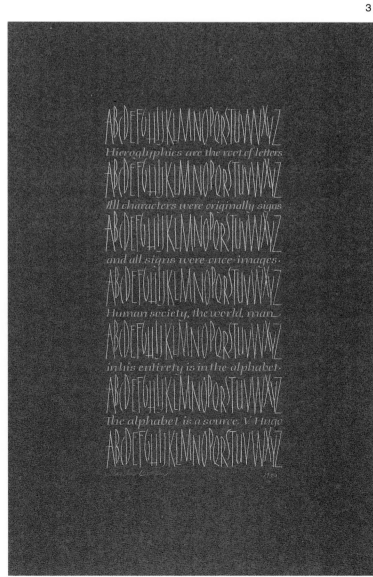

1

Timothy Botts. *Chicago Winter*, 1991. 12 x 18. Oriental brush, gouache, on handmade paper. Vol. 9, # 4, Summer 1992.
Text: "Here's Chicago" by Patrick M. Hartnett.

2

Mike Kecseg. *The Chicago Fire*, 1991. 49 x 20. Pointed pen, gouache on Canson paper. *1992 Annual*.
Text: Various newspaper reports.

3

Marsha Brady. *The Alphabet is a Source...* 1991. 13¼ x 19½. Speedball B nib, Brause nibs, gouache, dry pigment on Larroque paper. Author: Victor Hugo. *1991 Annual*.

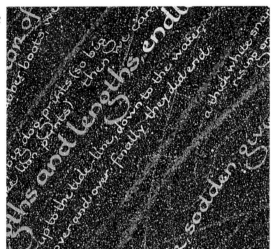

1-2
Barbara J. Bruene. *March*, 1991. 30 x 12. Metal nibs, colored pencil, watercolor, gouache, oil pastel on 140 lb. cold press watercolor paper.
1992 Annual.
Text: "The End of March" by Elizabeth Bishop.

3-4
Sheila Waters. *Tor House*, 1988. 24 x 18. Mitchell and Speedball C nibs, Chinese stick ink, on natural-toned calfskin vellum. Heading embellished with shell gold. Author: Robinson Jeffers. Photographed by Peter Waters.
1989 Annual.

5
Donald Jackson. *And He Shall Send His Angels*, 1988. 9⅜ x 7½. Vellum, stained with red and blue water-based lino-printing ink applied with a roller. Written and decorated with gouache, raised and burnished gold and powder gold. In places the gold leaf has been burnished directly onto vellum. Collection of Carol Pallesen Hicks. Vol. 6, #2, Winter 1988.

AND THEN SHALL APPEAR
THE SIGN OF THE SON OF MAN IN HEAVEN:
AND THEN
ALL THE TRIBES
OF THE EARTH
SHALL MOURN.

·AND·HE·SHALL·SEND·
HIS·ANGELS·

WITH A GREAT SOUND OF A
TRUMPET AND THEY SHALL GATHER
THE ELECT FROM THE FOUR WINDS,

S·MATTHEW·XXIV
3031

5

4

COME IN THE MORNING
YOU WILL SEE WHITE GULLS
WEAVING A DANCE OVER BLUE WATER
THE WANE OF THE MOON
THEIR DANCE-COMPANION.
A GHOST WALKING
BY DAYLIGHT,
BUT WILDER AND WHITER THAN
ANY BIRD IN THE WORLD.
MY GHOST YOU NEEDN'T LOOK FOR;
IT IS PROBABLY
HERE, BUT A DARK ONE,
DEEP IN THE GRANITE,
NOT DANCING ON WIND
WITH THE MAD WINGS AND THE DAY MOON

1

Anna Wolf. *Letter Labyrinth,* 1991. 18 x 24. Metallic markers, white Pentel Correction Pen, on Strathmore charcoal paper. Photographed by Charles Kennard. Vol. 9, #2, Winter 1992.

2

Carl E. Kurtz. *Memorial to Richard Matthews #17,* 1984. 30 x 22. Gillott nibs, oil based paint, gouache on Fabriano paper. Author: Cesare Pavese. Vol. 7, #1, Fall 1989.

3

Terry Englehart. *Eurydice #1,* 1991. 22 x 30. Ruling pen, ink, watercolor paper. *1992 Annual.*

Text: "Eurydice" by Edith Sitwell.

1

Malla 87

AND THE ANGEL THAT TALKED WITH ME CAME BACK AND WALKED ME, AS A MAN THAT IS WAKENED OUT OF HIS SLEEP, AND HE SAID TO ME, WHAT SEEST THOU & AND I SAID I HAVE LOOKED AND BEHOLD A CANDLESTICK ALL OF GOLD, WITH A BOWL UPON THE TOP OF IT & SEVEN LAMPS & SEVEN PIPES TO THE SEVEN LAMPS & I ASKED, WHAT ARE THESE & THE ANGEL SAID, THIS IS THE WORD OF THE LORD TO ZERUBBAVEL & A OLIVE TREE ON EACH SIDE OF THE BOWL

לא בחיל ולא בכח
כי אם־ברוחי אמר ד׳ צבאות
NOT BY MIGHT, NOR BY POWER,   BUT BY MY SPIRIT, SAYS THE LORD OF HOSTS ❧
THE VISION OF ZECHARIAH , 4 : 1-6

1
Malla Carl. *Vision of Zechariah,* 1987. 21½ x 31. Sofer's (Scribe's) ink,
India ink, flat gilding on a gum ammoniac base on vellum. Photographed by
David Harris, Jerusalem. *1989 Annual.*
Text: Zechariah 4:1-7.
2
Terry Louie. *Hua Flower,* 1990. 32 x 20. Wolf-hair brush, Chinese stick ink
on bark speckled rice paper. Photographed by Alan Chiu. *1991 Annual.*
3
Carl E. Kurtz. *Dance of Character: Sedately Grave,* 1991. 22 x 30. Frisket
film cut with knife, acrylic paint, airbrush on Strathmore paper. *1992 Annual.*

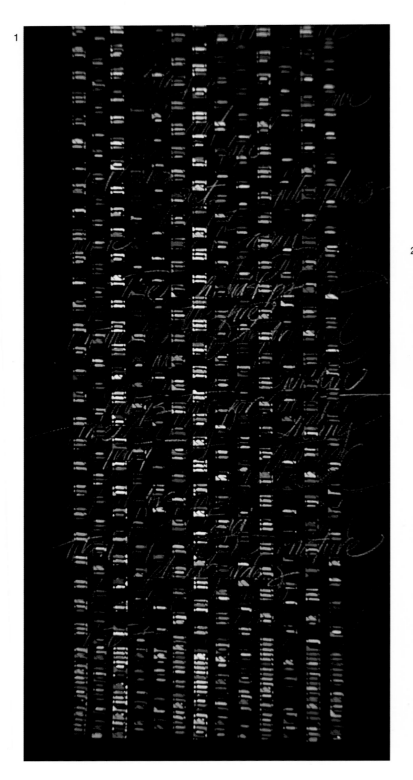

1
Elaine M. Grohman. *Untitled Woven I,* 1990. 16½ x 29. Prismacolor
pencils, ink on Canson Mi Tientes paper. Vol. 8, #2, Winter 1990.
2
Guillermo Rodriguez-Benitez. *Madrugada*, 1975. 60' x 17'. Tapestry. Client:
Puerto Rico Convention Center. Detail of the full tapestry which appeared in
Vol. 7, #34, Summer 1990.
Text: Poem by Louis Llorens Torres.
3
Jean Evans. *AM: 1979*. 5 x 7. Watercolor and Sumi ink. Vol. 5, #1, Winter
1988.

181

1

Ward Dunham. *Merton Gorby,* 1991. 31 x 47. Black and vermillion Chinese inks, cadmium red deep and alizarin crimson gouache, and wine on hand-made Twinrocker bleached Abaca paper. Client: Jerry Gorby. *1992 Annual.*
Text: "A Trappist Monk" by Thomas Merton.

2

Ward Dunham. *The Scum Also Rises,* 1989. 30 x 47. Chinese ink, black and vermillion on Twinrocker bleached Abaca paper. Author: Ernest Hemingway. Client: Brooks, Collins and Deana Jay Chu Nim.
1990 Annual.

3-4

Nancy R. Leavitt. *The Painted Road,* 1992. 6¾ x 9½. Metal nibs, brushes, gouache, watercolor, glair, on lithographed Rives lightweight paper.
#3 Author: Arthur Miller, appeared in the *1992 Annual.*
#4 Text: Jumbled Alphabet.

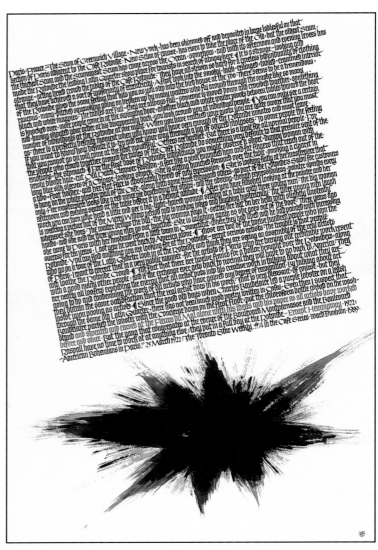

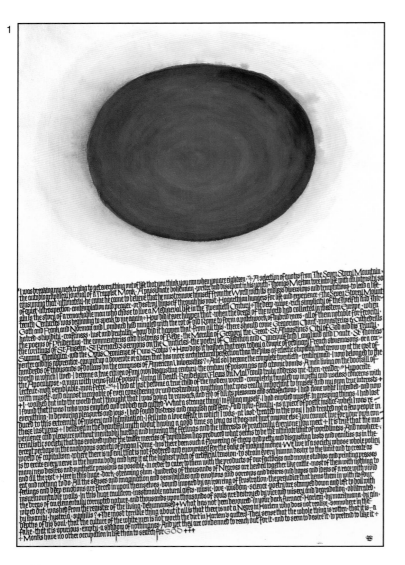

3

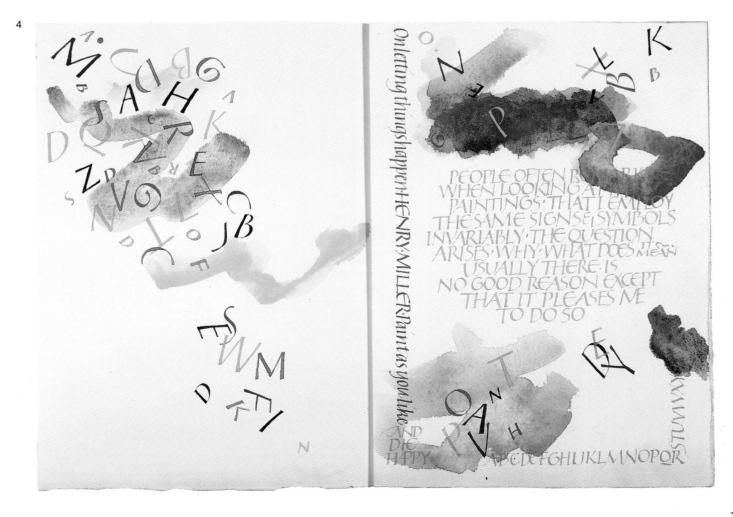

4

On letting things happen·HENRY·MILLER·Paint as you like

PEOPLE OFTEN REMARK
WHEN LOOKING AT MY
PAINTINGS·THAT I EMPLOY
THE SAME SIGNS & SYMBOLS
INVARIABLY·THE QUESTION
ARISES·WHY·WHAT DOES IT MEAN
USUALLY THERE IS
NO GOOD REASON EXCEPT
THAT IT PLEASES ME
TO DO SO

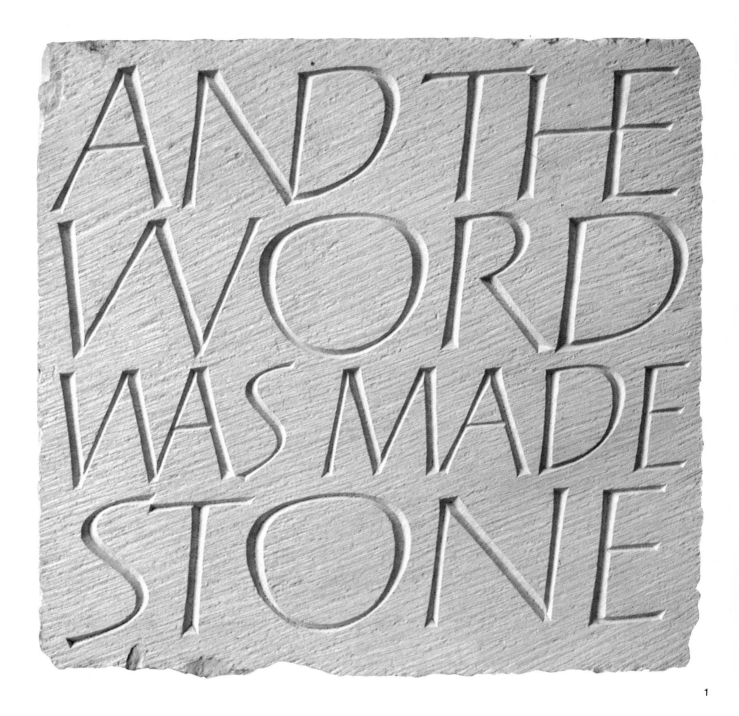

1
Tom Perkins. *And the Word was Made Stone*, 1990. 12½ x 12½. Letters incised with a mallet and chisel, surface left with a chiseled texture, French limestone. *1992 Annual*.
Text: From an Essay on Eric Gill, by his friend, the Painter & Poet, David Jones.
2
Derick Pao. *abc*, 1984. 3½ x 3¼ (plate size). Original: Fountain pen on textured paper. Blind embossed on handmade paper. Vol. 8, #4, Summer 1991.
3
Mary White. *Calligraphic Marks*, 1992. 32 cm. diameter. Wide-flanged bowl, thrown, brushed black oxide under barium glaze. In the permanent collection of the Gutenberg Museum, Mainz, Germany. Vol. 7, #4, Summer 1990.
Text: *The Waves* by Virginia Woolf. Used by permission of the Literary Estate of Virginia Woolf and the Hogarth Press.

THE SKY EXCEPT THAT THE SEA THE SUN HAD NOT YET RISEN THE SEA WAS
WHITENED: WAS SLIGHTLY CREASED AS IF A CLOTH HAD
THE SKY VIRGINIA WOLF· A DARK LINE LAY ON THE HORIZON DIVIDING
ONLY AS THE SKY· THE SEA WAS INDISTINGUISHABLE FROM
THE SKY· WRINKLES IN THE SEA WAS INDISTINGUISHABLE FROM
THE SEA FROM THE SKY· ONLY AS THE GREY CLOTH· GRAND WRINKLES IN IT GRAND

3

2

1
Emily Brown Shields. *Composers Bowl*, 1986. 10½ diameter x 9¾ high.
Original: Speedball pen and ink on paper. Lettering sandblasted onto glass.
Client: Steuben Glass. Glass designed by David Dowler. Photographed by
Robert Moore. Vol. 4, #1, Fall 1986.
2
St. Clair Richard. *Ice Palace*, 1985. 14 high. Diamond scriber on hand-
blown crystal. Photographed by Bob Kodadek. Collection of Charles Pearce.
Vol. 5, #2, Winter 1987.

BIBLIOGRAPHY

Camp, Ann. *Pen Lettering.* 5th ed. Dryad Press, Leicester, 1978.

Catich, Edward M. *Reed, Pen, & Brush Alphabets for Writing and Lettering.* Hastings House Publishers, New York, 1980.

Catich, Edward M.. *The Origin of the Serif.* The Catfish Press, St. Ambrose College, Davenport, Iowa, 1968.

Child, Heather. *Calligraphy Today.* Revised ed. Cassell & Collier Macmillan Publishers Limited, London, 1963; Pentalic Corporation, New York, 1976.

Davis, Susan (ed.). *International Calligraphy Today.* Watson-Guptill Publications, New York, 1982.

Fairbank, Alfred. *A Book of Scripts.* Penguin Books Limited, Harmondsworth, 1949; Faber and Faber Limited, London, 1977.

Fink, Joanne and Kastin, Judy (ed.s). *The Speedball Textbook, 22d Edition.* Hunt Manufacturing Co., North Carolina, 1991.

Folsom, Rose. *The Calligraphers' Dictionary.* Thames and Hudson Ltd, London, 1990.

Harris, David. *Calligraphy: Modern Masters - Art, Inspiration, and Technique.* Crescent Books, New York, 1991.

Harvey, Michael. *Calligraphy in the Graphic Arts.* The Bodley Head Limited, London, 1988.

Hoefer, Karlgeorg. *Kalligraphie.* ECON Taschenbuch Verlag, Dusseldorf, 1986.

Jackson, Donald. *The Story of Writing.* Taplinger Publishing Company, New York, 1981.

Jackson, Martin. *Modern Scribes and Lettering Artists.* Taplinger Publishing Company, New York, 1980.

Johnston, Edward. *Writing & Illuminating, & Lettering.* 32d ed., reprint ed. Pitman Publishing Limited, London, 1906; Taplinger Publishing Company, New York, 1978.

Society of Scribes and Illuminators. *Contemporary Calligraphy: Modern Scribes and Lettering Artists II.* Taplinger Publishing Company, New York, 1986.

Switkin, Abraham. *Hand Lettering Today.* Harper & Row, New York, 1976.

Zapf, Hermann. *Hermann Zapf and His Design Philosophy.* Society of Typographic Arts, Chicago, 1987.

Appendix I Calligraphy Societies

Alpha Beta Club
PO Box 73615
Kowloon Central Post Office
Hong Kong

Australian Society of Calligraphy
PO Box 184
N.S.W., 2114 Australia

Big Sky Scribes
1610 Boulder Avenue
Helena, MT 59601

Bow Valley Calligraphy Guild
PO Box 1647, Station M
Calgary, Alberta T2P 2L7 Canada

Bund Deutcher Buchkunstler
6050 Offenbach Am Main
Herrnstrawse, 81 West Germany

Calligraphers' Guild
PO Box 304
Ashland, OR 97520

The Calligraphers Guild
PO Box 551
Crugers, NY 10521

Calligraphers Guild of Jacksonville
PO Box 5873
Jacksonville, FL 32247

Calligraphers of Maine
PO Box 2751
South Portland, ME 04106

Calligraphers Guild of New Haven
PO Box 2099
Short Beach, CT 06405

Calligraphers Guild of Northern Pennsylvania
209 Carnation Drive
Clarks Summit, PA 18411

Calligraphers Guild of Ottawa
1941 Bel-Air Drive
Ottawa K2C 0X1 Canada

Calligraphers Guild of the Peninsula
PO Box 5031
Newport News, VA 23605

The Calligraphers Guild of Amsterdam
c/o Margot Freeman
20 Lindbergh Avenue
Amsterdam, NY 12010

Calligraphic Arts Guild of Sacramento
PO Box 161976
Sacramento, CA 95816

Calligraphic Arts Guild of Toronto
PO Box 115, Willowdale Station "A"
North York, Ontario M2N 5S7 Canada

Calligraphic Society of Arizona
PO Box 27695
Tempe, AZ 85282

Calligraphy & Italic Handwriting Society
Box 34481
Jeppestown, Johannesburg, 2043 South Africa

Calligraphy Guild of Chattanooga
PO Box 15164
Chattanooga, TN 37415

Calligraphy Guild of Columbus
PO Box 14184
Columbus, OH 43214

The Calligraphy Guild of Manitoba
PO Box 2191
Winnipeg, MB R3C 3R5 Canada

The Calligraphy Guild of Oklahoma
PO Box 33098
Tulsa, OK 74135

Calligraphy Guild of Pittsburgh
PO Box 8167
Pittsburgh, PA 15217

The Calligraphy Society of Victoria
PO Box 2623W, Gpo Melbourne
Victoria, 3001 Australia

Capital Calligraphers
PO Box 17284
Salem, OR 97305

Capital City Scribes
PO Box 5427
Austin, TX 78763

Carolina Lettering Arts Society
PO Box 20466
Raleigh, NC 27619

Center for Calligraphic Arts
PO Box 8005
Wichita, KS 67208

Chicago Calligraphy Collective
c/o Jane Carlson
22W070 Stratford Court
Glen Ellyn, IL 60137

Chinook Calligraphy Guild
2609 14th Avenue North
Lethbridge, Alberta T1H 4C8 Canada

Colleagues of Calligraphy
PO Box 4024
St. Paul, MN 55104-0024

Colorado Calligraphers' Guild
PO Box 6746, Cherry Creek Station
Denver, CO 80209

Concord Scribes
PO Box 405
Concord, MA 01742

Connecticut Valley Calligraphers
PO Box 1122
Farmington, CT 06034

Corpus Christi Calligraphers
5813 Limerick
Corpus Christi, TX 78413

Cream City Calligraphers
PO Box 1468
Milwaukee, WI 53201-1468

Cursive Italic Handwriting
PO Box 92
Aberdeen, MD 21001

The Delaware Calligraphy Guild
81 Red Mill Road
Newark, DE 19711-6667

Delta Scribes
PO Box 3272
Vanderbijlpark 1900 South Africa

Edmonton Calligraphic Society
Box 336, 9768-170 Street
Edmonton, Alberta T5T 5L4 Canada

Escribiente
PO Drawer 26718
Albuquerque, NM 87125

Fairbank Calligraphy Society
c/o 80 Howe Street
Victoria, BC V8V 4K3 Canada

Fort Worth Calligraphers Guild
PO Box 101732
Fort Worth, TX 76185

Friends of Calligraphy
PO Box 5194
San Francisco, CA 94101

Friends of the Alphabet
PO Box 11764
Atlanta, GA 30355

Genesee Valley Calligraphy Guild
55 Monteroy Road
Rochester, NY 14618

Guild of the Golden Quill
PO Box 1221
Dayton, OH 45401-1221

Hamilton Calligraphy Guild
PO Box 57144, Jackson Station
2 King Street West
Hamilton, Ontario L8P 4W9 Canada

The Houston Calligraphy Guild
c/o The Art League of Houston
1953 Montrose Boulevard
Houston, TX 77006

The Int. Assoc. of Master Penmen & Teachers
2213 Arlington Avenue
Middletown, OH 45042

Island Scribes
PO Box 1043, North Baldwin Station
Baldwin, NY 11510-1043

Jersey Shore Calligraphers' Guild
PO Box 123
Highlands, NJ 07732

Kalligrafia vzw
Catershoflaan 19
B-2170 Merksem
Belgium

Kalligraphos, The Dallas Calligraphy Society
6660 Santa Anita Drive
Dallas, TX 75214

Kentuckiana Calligraphy Guild
PO Box 194
New Albany, IN 47150-0194

La Societe des Calligraphes
PO Box 704, Snowdon Station
Montreal, Quebec H3X 3X8 Canada

Lettering Arts Guild of Boston
PO Box 461
Boston, MA 02102

Memphis Calligraphy Guild
4752 Linda Lane
Memphis, TN 38117

The Mercator Society
Rembrandtstraat 3
2712 SE Zoetermeer Holland

Michigan Association of Calligraphers
PO Box 55
Royal Oak, MI 48068-0055

Missoula Calligraphers Guild
213 West Beckwith
Missoula, MT 59801-3826

Mysticalligraphers
PO Box 267
Mystic, CT 06355

New Orleans Lettering Arts Association
PO Box 4117
New Orleans, LA 70178-4117

North Country Calligraphy Guild
PO Box 1023
Vista, CA 92085-1023

Northern Lights Calligraphers
PO Box 6220
Fort McMurray, Alberta T9W 4W1 Canada

Northern Utah Association of Calligraphers
1446 North 1640 East
Logan, UT 84321

The Octavo Society
2815 Woody Drive
Billings, MT 59102

Opulent Order of Practicing Scribes
PO Box 743
Roswell, NM 88201

The Ozark Society of Scribes
PO Box 451
Eureka Springs, AR 72632

Pacific Scribes
PO Box 3392
Santa Clara, CA 95055

Pen Crafters Guild of El Paso
10152 Buckwood Avenue
El Paso, TX 79925

Pen Dragons
PO Box 327
Afton, MN 55001-0327

Philadelphia Calligraphers Society
PO Box 7174
Elkins Park, PA 19117-0174

Piedmont Society of Scribes
PO Box 589
Winston-Salem, NC 27102

The Portland Society for Calligraphy
PO Box 4621
Portland, OR 97208

The Quilligraphers' Guild
PO Box 126
Leicester, MA 01524-0126

San Antonio Calligraphers Guild
PO Box 6476
San Antonio, TX 78209

San Diego Fellow Calligraphers
PO Box 84960
San Diego, CA 92138-4960

The Scribes of Central Florida
PO Box 1753
Winter Park, FL 32790-1753

Scriptores
Postbus 331
9100 Ah Dokkum The Netherlands

Scripts & Scribes of Summit County
3402 Ridgewood Road
Akron, OH 44313

Skagit Whatcom Calligraphers
1233 Field Road
Bow, WA 98232

The Society for Calligraphy
PO Box 64174
Los Angeles, CA 90064

Society for Calligraphy and Handwriting
PO Box 31963
Seattle, WA 98103

The Society for Italic Handwriting
"Highfields" Nightingale Road
Secretary: J. Fricker
Guildford, Surrey GU1 1ER England

Society of Desert Scribes
PO Box 19524
Las Vegas, NV 89132

Society of Scribes & Illuminators
54 Boileau Road
London, SW 13 9BL England

Society of Scribes. Ltd.
PO Box 933
New York, NY 10150

Sooner Scribes
PO Box 312
Norman, OK 73070

South Florida Calligraphy Guild
1900 Sabal Palm Drive, #401
Fort Lauderdale, FL 33324

St. Louis Calligraphy Guild
PO Box 16563
St. Louis, MO 63105

St. Petersburg Society of Scribes
2960 58th Avenue South
St. Petersburg, FL 33712

Suffolk Scribes
PO Box 433
Bellport, NY 11713-0433

Suncoast Scribes
c/o Betty Cohane
3113 Cambridge Avenue
Bradenton, FL 33507

Tacoma Calligraphy Guild
PO Box 851
Tacoma, WA 98401

Tidewater Calligraphy Guild
PO Box 8871
Virginia Beach, VA 23450

Valley Calligraphy Guild
2352 Van Ness
Eugene, OR 97403

Village Calligraphers Guild
PO Box 194
Jamison, PA 18929

Washington Calligraphers Guild
PO Box 3688
Merrifield, VA 22116-3688

Westcoast Calligraphy Society
#604-2020 Fullerton Avenue
North Vancouver, BC V7P 3G3

The Western Reserve Calligraphers
PO Box 110686
Cleveland, OH 44111-0686

Wisconsin Calligraphers
2124 Kendall A
Madison, WI 53705-3916

Write-On Calligraphers
PO Box 277
Edmonds, WA 98020

Wyoming Scribes
507 South 7th
Laramie, WY 82070

Calligraphy Review
1624 24th Avenue SW
Norman, OK 73072
800-348-PENS
405-364-8914 FAX

Appendix II Contributors

Adams, Cheryl O.
2124 NW 139th Street
Des Moines, IA 50325

Alice
221 East 88th Street
New York, NY 10128

Amarotico, Diane
PO Box 239
Plumsteadville, PA 18949

Bar-Menachem, Luba
74 Habad Street
Jerusalem, Israel

Barnes, Michele D.
357 Foch Boulevard
Mineola, NY 11501

Beasley, Dick (*Estate of*)
c/o June Beasley
1822 North Beaver Street
Flagstaff, AZ 86001

Bell, Jill
1916 C Farrell Avenue
Redondo Beach, CA 90278

Bernd, Adolf
Wilhelm-Raabe Strasse 20
3252 Bad Munder 1
Germany

Blackman, Alan
4119 24th Street
San Francisco, CA 94114

Bloch, Anthony
854 West 181st Street, #6D
New York, NY 10033

Botts, Timothy R.
367 Oak Street
Glen Ellyn, IL 60137

Boyajian, Robert
511 Third Avenue, #4D
New York, NY 10016

Brady, Lawrence R.
11561 Harrisburg Road
Los Alamitos, CA 90720

Brady, Marsha
11561 Harrisburg Road
Los Alamitos, CA 90720

Bringham, Sherry
1804 Arlington Boulevard
El Cerrito, CA 94530

Broide, Lynn
1030 NW McNiel Avenue
Lawrence, NY 11559

Brown, Denis
6 Meadow Avenue
Dundrum, Dublin 16
Ireland

Bruene, Professor Barbara J.
Gallery Director
Iowa State University
2122 Greeley Street
Ames, IA 50010

Burgert, Hans-Joachim
Lassenstr. 22
1000 Berlin-33
Germany

Carl, Malla
20 Keren-Kayemet
92465 Jerusalem, Israel

Carlson, Peg
2123 Mississippi Boulevard
Bettendorf, IA 52722

Carney, Marijo A.
2256 Tipperary Road
Kalamazoo, MI 49008

Cicale, Annie
68 Sigman Road
Fletcher, NC 28732

Clark, Michael
2903 Kenwood Avenue
Richmond, VA 23228

Cohen, Avraham
Avco Graphics
3313 Shelburne Road
Baltimore, MD 21208

Curry, Jocelyn
103 NW 200th Street
Seattle, WA 98177

Cusick, Rick
7501 Westgate
Lenaxa, KS 66216

Deaver, Georgia
1045 Sansome Street, #311
San Francisco, CA 94111

Devaux, Ludo
Van Dornestraat 3
2100 Antwerp-Deurne
Belgium

Dieterich A., Claude
831 Adams Street, #3
Albany, CA 94706

Dill, Jane
123 Townsend Street, #525
San Francisco, CA 94107

Dubay, Inga S.
1805 NW 34th Avenue
Portland, OR 97201

Dunham, A. Ward
PO Box 330138
San Francisco, CA 94133

Eldridge, Keith
320 St. George Street
Sussex NB
Canada EOE 1PO

Engelbrecht, Lisa
6329 Mariouita Street
Long Beach, CA 90803

Englehart, Terry
40353 Oakmore Road
Oakland, CA 94602

Epstein, Glen
1315 Muscatine Avenue
Iowa City, IA 52240

Erickson, Carol
1738 NW 143 Avenue
Portland, OR 97229

Evans, Jean
142 Garden Street
Cambridge, MA 02138

Ezell, Reggie
2643 North Kimball
Chicago, IL 60647

Faulk, Holly Sanford
14 Morton Street
New York, NY 10014

Fay, Leana
620 Reasor Drive
Virginia Beach, VA 23464

Fink, Joanne
Calligrapher's Ink, Ltd.
345 Eden Trail
Lake Mary, FL 32746

Formo, Jean
3429 Richmond Avenue
Shoreview, MN 55126

Forst, Siegmund
170 Rodney Street
Brooklyn, NY 11211

Frank, Eugene
7410 Poplar Drive
Forestville, CA 95436

Gatti, David
40 View Acre Drive
Huntington, NY 11743

Gattman, Leslie
7410 Poplar Drive
Forestville, CA 95436

Glasser, Howard
28 Forge Road
Assonet, MA 02702

Groat, Jenny Hunter
PO Box 295
Lagunitas, CA 94938

Grohman, Elaine M.
Grohman's Studio
28403 Alice Kay
Farmington Hills, MI 48334

Haanes, Christopher
Kalligrafi
Hesselbergsgt.3
0555 Oslo, Norway

Hansson, Lennart
Stora Nygatan 75
S-21137 Malmo
Sweden

Herrera, Paul P.
2123 Mississippi Boulevard
Bettendorf, IA 52722

Hoefer, Prof. Karlgeorg
D-6050 Offenbach A. Main
Weilburger Weg 7
Germany

Hughey, Michael W.
PO Box 18122
Ashville, NC 28814

Ingmire, Thomas
1040-A Filbert
San Francisco, CA 94133

Jackson, Donald
Calligraphy Centre
The Hendre Monmouth Gwent
United Kingdom

Jackson, Martin
2065 Creelman Avenue
Vancouver, BC V6J 1C2 Canada

Jacobson, Cheryl
510 Grant Street
Iowa City, IA 52240

Johnson, Iskra
1605 12th, #26
Seattle, WA 98122

Jones, Stan A.
3996 West 16th Avenue
Vancouver, BC V6R 3C8 Canada

Kadin, Ted Simcha
1507 38th Street, #1F
Brooklyn, NY 11218

Kastin, Judy
603 Bond Court
Merrick, NY 11566

Katz, Sivia
5403 Vicaris Street
Philadelphia, PA 19128

Kecseg, Michael
4022 North Major Avenue
Chicago, IL 60634

Kelly, Jerry
20 West 9th Street
New York, NY 10011

Kelly, Rosemary T.
675 Heritage Drive, 7-108
Hoffman Estates, IL 60194

Kotin, Rory
324 East 84th Street, #3C
New York, NY 10028

Kurtz, Carl E.
1325 Wornall Road
Excelsior Springs, MO 64024

Larcher, Jean
16 Chemin des Bourgognes
95000 Cergy
France

Leavitt, Nancy R.
PO Box 330
6 Spring Street
Stillwater, ME 04489

Levine, Linda
8710 Braeburn Drive
Annandale, VA 22003

Louie, Terry
3550 19th Street
San Francisco, CA 94110

Lundquist, Linnea
PO Box 330138
San Francisco, CA 34133

Mackechnie, Anne V.
PO Box 16
Nicholasville, KY 40340

Madaki, Abdul Lateef
PO Box 1887
Peter Stuyvesant Station
New York, NY 10009

Margulies, Henry
12 Saul Place
Plainview, New York 11803

McKee, Elizabeth
H53, Rd. 82
Gulshan, Dhaka 1212
Bangladesh

Millner, C.A.
94 Union Street
Norfolk, MA 02056

Monroe, Holly
514 Lakeridge Drive
Cincinnati, OH 45231

Morentz, Barry
320 East 23rd Street
New York, NY 10010

Mueller, Judy
246 Roslyn Street
Rochester, NY 14619

O'Brian, Mary Lou
770 Tiffany Drive
Gaithersburg, MD 20878

Overley, Jill
285 East 38th Avenue
Eugene, OR 94705

Pao, Derick
Lettering Dept.
American Greetings
10500 American Road
Cleveland, OH 44144

Paschke, Chris A.
Designs Ink
2 Klarides Village 102
Seymour, CT 06483

Perkins, Tom
40 High Street
Cambs. CBG 2RB
England

Pieper, Katharina
Herzogstrasse 24
D-6650 Homburg-Jagersburg
Germany

Pinto, Anna
929 Willow Avenue
Hoboken, NJ 07030

Pronenko, Leonid
350065 Krasnodov
Nerkipelova Street, 15-67
Russia

Reaves, Marilyn
1260 West 15th Avenue, #6
Eugene, OR 97402

Richard, Chava Wolpert
c/o Artist Studio Centers, Inc.
1651 Third Avenue
New York, NY 10128

Richard, St. Clair
360 Van Duzer Street
Staten Island, NY 10304

Robinson, Marcy
Building 3, #1G
181 River Road
Nutley, NJ 07110

Rodriguez-Benitez, Guillermo *(Estate of)*
450 Ponce de Leon Avenue
San Juan, Puerto Rico 00901

Rohrs, Carl
228 Ocean View
Santa Cruz, CA 95062

Rosen, Myrna P.
6362 Phillips Avenue
Pittsburgh, PA 15217

Rosenberg, Carol
11637 Forest Point Road
Strongsville, OH 44136

Rosenstein, Mordecai
7850 Montgomery Avenue
Elkins Park, PA 19117

Saucier, Linda
c/o Gay Ayers
18 Elizabeth Road
Farmington, CT 06032

Scott-Morris, Alice
Daydream Graphics
22715 Clarendon Street
Woodland Hills, CA 91867

Shaw, Paul
785 West End Avenue
New York, NY 10025

Shields, Emily Brown
3251 42nd Street
Long Island City, NY 11103

Skaggs, Steven
415 Trinity Hills Lane
Louisville, KY 40207

Skarsgard, Susan
807 Hutchins Avenue
Ann Arbor, MI 48103

Stentz, Nancy
Nancy Stentz Design
87 Wall Street
Seattle, WA 98181

Stevens, John
53 Clearmeadow Drive
East Meadow, NY 11554

Tresser, Jerry
4 Stacy Court
Port Jefferson, NY 11777

Van Stone, Mark
3422 SE Grant Court
Portland, OR 97214

van Slingerland, Elmo
Burgemeester Baumannlaan, #62C
3043 AN Rotterdam
Holland

Vick, Gail
55 Monteroy Road
Rochester, NY 14168

von Arx, Diane M.
3340 Bryant Avenue South
Minneapolis, MN 55408

Walton, Brenda
14 Midway Court
Sacramento, CA 95817

Waters, Julian
23707 Woodfield Road
Gaithersburg, MD 20882

Weinberg, Elana
509 West 110th Street
New York, NY 10025

Weisberg, Patricia
382 Central Park West, #16V
New York, NY 10025

White, Mary
Zimmerplatzweg 6
Wonsheim
Germany

Wimberly, Jannell K.
2621 Pin Oak Lane
Plano, TX 75075

Winn-Lederer, Ilene
986 Lilac Street
Pittsburgh, PA 15217

Winters, Eleanor
245 Warren Street
Brooklyn, NY 11201

Wolf, Anna
2214 Los Angeles Avenue
Berkeley, CA 94707

Index

Acknowledgments

We wish to thank everyone who submitted work for *Lettering Arts*.
Without their enthusiasm and cooperation, this book would not have been possible.
We also wish to thank our editor, Susan Kapsis, and our supportive families.

Our deep appreciation to Karyn Gilman,
Janet Hoffberg, Judy Mueller, John Stevens
and Sheila Waters for their invaluable help and advice.

Joanne Fink and Judy Kastin
Bellmore, New York